Carol Ann Tomlinson
Caroline Cunningham Eidson

Differentiation in Practice

A RESOURCE GUIDE FOR DIFFERENTIATING CURRICULUM

Grades K–5

ASCD

Association for Supervision and Curriculum Development
Alexandria, Virginia USA

Association for Supervision and Curriculum Development
1703 N. Beauregard St. • Alexandria, VA 22311-1714 USA
Telephone: 800-933-2723 or 703-578-9600 • Fax: 703-575-5400
Web site: http://www.ascd.org • E-mail: member@ascd.org

Gene R. Carter, *Executive Director;* Nancy Modrak, *Director of Publishing;* Julie Houtz, *Director of Book Editing & Production;* Katie Martin, *Project Manager;* Georgia McDonald, *Senior Graphic Designer;* Valerie Sprague, *Desktop Publisher.*

All Web links in this book are correct as of the publication date below but may have become inactive or otherwise modified since that time. If you notice a deactivated or changed link, please e-mail books@ascd.org with the words "Link Update" in the subject line. In your message, please specify the Web link, the book title, and the page number on which the link appears.

Printed in the United States of America.

s6/03

ASCD product no.: 102294
ASCD member price: $21.95   nonmember price: $25.95

Library of Congress Cataloging-in-Publication Data
Tomlinson, Carol A.
   Differentiation in practice: a resource guide for differentiating
curriculum, grades K-5 / Carol Ann Tomlinson and Caroline Cunningham
Eidson.
      p. cm.
Includes bibliographical references and index.
   ISBN 0-87120-760-5 (alk. paper)
  1. Education, Elementary—United States—Curricula. 2. Individualized
instruction—United States. I. Eidson, Caroline Cunningham, 1968- II.
Title.

   LB1570.T593 2003
   372.19—dc21

13 12 11 10 09 08 07 06 05 04 03   12 11 10 9 8 7 6 5 4 3 2 1

For the students
who sometimes gently and sometimes
ferociously insisted we see them as individuals

✳

For mentors
who made us believe it was not only possible
but necessary to do so

✳

For colleagues
who share a passion for education as a shared enterprise
that enables students and teachers to grow together

✳

And for family and friends
who renew our energy and greet us with joy—
whether or not we get it right.

Differentiation in Practice

A Resource Guide for Differentiating Curriculum, Grades K–5

Acknowledgments

No book of this sort is ever really written by just one or two people. There are many hands, minds, and professional practices reflected in its pages—and, therefore, many people to thank.

Our thanks foremost to the contributing authors of the units contained in this book: Jennifer Ann Bonnett, Elizabeth Hargrave, Laura Massey, and Sandra Williams Page. Each of them is the kind of educator who enhances not just the lives of students, but the lives of colleagues as well. They are able practitioners of differentiation and fine curriculum designers. In addition, they were willing to risk sharing their ideas—first with authors and editors, whom they knew would tinker with the material they submitted, and then with the teachers who would read the finished product and (quite rightly) examine each unit with a questioning eye. On behalf of all educators who learn from this book, our thanks to these talented teachers for making it happen.

We are indebted, too, to Cindy Strickland—a top-quality teacher, thinker, and editor—who edited, revised, and stretched our work. Her keen eye and solid thinking have made the book stronger in so many ways.

As always, the ASCD team of editors and designers were the best support system authors can hope for. The ASCD vision for and commitment to the concept of differentiation provides rich and fertile soil for this body of work. That ASCD staff members hold high standards for themselves encourages us always to do the same.

Both of this book's authors have become better educators in the partnership of colleagues. The teachers with whom we taught longest (particularly those in Fauquier County, Virginia, and at Peabody School in Charlottesville, Virginia) have been catalysts for our own professional growth. We're also nourished by educators from around the country who ask hard questions and generously share their work—both the successes and the setbacks.

Our friends and families support the time-intensive goal of writing, even at the expense of more carefree weekends, holidays, and vacations. It would be difficult to overstate the role of that sort of partnership in our mission.

Finally, both of us are teachers. The faces and lives of the young learners we once taught continue to steer us today. The collegiality of the adults we now teach helps us keep theory and practice—the cornerstones of effective educational writing—in balance. Both groups remind us daily of the truth in Susan O'Hanian's observation about being an educator: First, no matter how much the educator does, it will never seem enough. Second, the educator's inability to do everything is not a license to do nothing. In that spirit, we thank all those who helped us take one more step in a progression of steps that has no end.

Introduction

This book is part of a series of ASCD publications on differentiating instruction. Each is designed to play a particular role in helping educators think about and develop classrooms that attend to learner needs as they guide learners through a curricular sequence.

How to Differentiate Instruction in Mixed-Ability Classrooms (Tomlinson, 2001) explains the basic framework of differentiation. Such a framework allows teachers to plan in consistent and coherent ways. *The Differentiated Classroom: Responding to the Needs of All Learners* (Tomlinson, 1999a) elaborates on the framework and describes classroom scenarios in which differentiation is taking place. A third book, *Leadership for Differentiating Schools and Classrooms* (Tomlinson & Allan, 2000), discusses how to link what we know about school change with the goals of differentiation and seeks to provide guidance for educational leaders who want to be a part of promoting and supporting responsive instruction. In addition to these books, an ASCD Professional Inquiry Kit called *Differentiating Instruction for Mixed-Ability Classrooms* (Tomlinson, 1996) guides educators, in an inductive manner, to explore and apply key principles of differentiation.

Four video programs, all produced by Leslie Kiernan and ASCD, give progressively expansive images of how differentiation actually looks in the classroom. *Differentiating Instruction* (1997) shows brief applications of differentiating content, process, and products according to student readiness, interest, and learning profile in primary, elementary, middle, and high school classrooms. It also illustrates a number of instructional strategies used for purposes of differentiating or modifying instruction. A three-video set, *At Work in the Differentiated Classroom* (2001), shows excerpts from a month-long unit in a middle school classroom as a means of exploring essential principles of differentiation, examines management in differentiated settings from primary grades through high school, and probes the role of the teacher in a differentiated classroom. *A Visit to a Differentiated Classroom* (2001) takes viewers through a single day in a multi-age, differentiated elementary classroom. Finally, *Instructional Strategies for the Differentiated Classroom* (2003) illustrates approaches to address varied learner needs and support responsive teaching. Each of these materials attempts to help educators think about the nature of classrooms that are defensibly differentiated and move toward development of such classrooms. Each of the publications plays a different role in the process of reflection, definition, and translation.

This book uses yet another lens to examine differentiation and support its implementation in classrooms. It joins a companion book (*Differentiation in Practice: A Resource Guide for Differentiating Curriculum, Grades 5–9*) in presenting a series of actual curricular units developed by teachers who work hard to differentiate instruction in their classrooms. Thus, these books move from defining and describing differentiation to providing the actual curriculum used to differentiate instruction.

Differentiation in the Elementary Years

Differentiating in elementary classrooms means that teachers proactively engage learners where they are, recognizing that an elementary classroom is a mixed bag of readiness levels, interests, and learning preferences. Anyone who has spent any time in a kindergarten classroom can attest that young children enter school at almost astoundingly different levels, with a wide variety of different interests and experiences, and with a broad range of learning preferences and styles. Just as in sports, where some students seem born to run, jump, and leap through games with ease while others struggle to walk a straight line, some students enter school ready to learn, having managed to already grasp the skills needed to do so. Other students take a while to warm up to the structure and requirements of school. And, while some differences among elementary students diminish as all are exposed to the same types of experiences and given

the same types of learning opportunities over time, other differences arise and become increasingly evident as students progress from grade to grade.

In elementary schools, the danger of "losing" students along the way is ever-present, and the same people who can attest to the wide range of differences among elementary students can also attest to the fact that students seem to be "checking out" of school and academics at earlier and earlier ages. For this reason, it becomes increasingly critical that elementary teachers find ways to encourage students to remain engaged in the learning process; this is a challenge that is difficult if not impossible to meet if students' differences are ignored.

Another reason why differentiation is so critical in the elementary years is that young students' early experiences have a profound impact on their views of school, their conceptions of the learning process, and their perceptions of themselves as learners. By igniting students' love of learning early in their schooling and by helping them to respect not only their own but also others' strengths, weaknesses, and interests, elementary school teachers establish the groundwork upon which students build their future learning. This book provides a vision of what student-responsive classrooms can look like during the elementary years in the hope that educators will continue to strive to instill in all learners a joy for learning and a love of the possibilities that it brings.

What the Book Is (and Isn't) Intended to Be

As we prepared to write this book and its companion (*Grades 5–9*), we had numerous conversations between ourselves, with editors, and with many colleagues in education. Each conversation helped us chart our eventual course. Our primary goal was to provide models of differentiated units of study. We wanted to move beyond (necessarily) episodic descriptions of differentiation to show how it might flow through an entire unit. We also wanted to present units at a range of grade levels and in a variety of subjects. It seemed too much to provide units for grades K–12 in a single book, so we began by working with units that span "the middle years." The book you're reading now adds differentiated units for grades K–5.

Even after narrowing the range of grade levels, we realized there were so many subjects to consider that we had to refine our focus further. Ultimately, we elected to include differentiated units in math (two units), science, social studies, and language arts (two units). And while we have developed the book with a primary and elementary focus, our intent is that it be useful to a broader range of teachers than the grade levels and subjects it specifically represents. This is a book designed to teach anyone who wants to learn how to differentiate curriculum how to do so—or how to do so more effectively.

To that end, each of the units is intended to be more representative than restrictive. That is, an elementary art teacher should be able to look at the social studies unit in this book, see how it works, and use similar principles and formats to develop a differentiated art unit for her students. A 7th grade language arts teacher should be able to study several of the units here and synthesize principles and procedures he finds therein to guide development of a differentiated language arts unit for 7th graders. In sum, we intend this book to be a vehicle for professional development.

What this book is *not* intended to be is off-the-shelf curriculum for any classroom. It is not possible to create the "correct" unit, for example, on how to teach about plants. Teachers in one

classroom will conceive that process differently than will teachers in other classrooms or teachers in a different part of the country, in a different type of school, or responsible for a different set of academic standards. In the end, then, we are presenting educators with a learning tool—not a teaching tool. If teachers (and other educators) can read this book and say, "There's something I can learn here," then we will have succeeded.

How the Book Is Designed

Because we want the book to be a learning tool for a maximum number of teachers, we have made key decisions about its presentation. First, we decided to begin the book with Part I's primer on differentiation—an essential piece for readers new to the topic and a helpful refresher for those already familiar with it. We also opted to include an extended glossary (page 184), which explains terms and strategies that might not be familiar to all readers. Collecting this information in the back of the book, we thought, was preferable to interrupting the units themselves with "sidebar" explanations.

Part II, the body of the book, is devoted to instructional units. We think it will be helpful to share some of our thinking about the layout and contents of the units, each of which is presented in four parts.

• **Unit Introduction.** The first component of every unit is the introduction, which includes a prose overview of the unit; a list of standards addressed in the unit; the key concepts and generalizations that help with teacher and student focus; a delineation of what students should know, understand, and be able to do as a result of the unit; and a list of the key instructional strategies used in the unit. Some of the units also make links across units and disciplines and promote connections with students' lives and experiences. Note that because of our desire to make the book a learning tool and not a set of lesson plans, we have listed the subject area for each unit, but not a grade level. Similarly, our references to the specific standards around which teachers constructed the units do not include grade-level designations.

• **Unit Overview Chart.** The second component is an overview chart, designed with three goals in mind: 1) to provide orientation in the form of a "big picture" snapshot of the unit's steps or events; 2) to provide an estimate of the amount of time each step or event requires; and 3) to clarify which portions of the unit apply to the class as a whole and which are differentiated.

• **Unit Description.** The third component is the unit description itself. It appears in the left-hand column of each unit page and gives a step-by-step explanation of what takes place in the classroom during the unit. Asterisks in the margins highlight differentiated components. All referenced supporting materials (samples such as worksheets, resource lists, learning contracts, graphic organizers, and assessments) appear at the end of the unit.

• **Teacher Commentary.** The fourth component is an explanation, in the voice of the teacher who created the unit, of what she was thinking as she planned and presented instruction. For our purposes, this is a particularly valuable element. To listen to the teacher who developed the unit is to move well beyond what happens in the classroom and to begin to analyze why teachers make decisions as they do. At one point in the writing and editing process, we thought we should reduce the teacher commentary sections to the fewest possible words; we quickly discovered that when we did so, we lost the magic the book has to offer. We hope

you enjoy listening to the teachers as much as we have.

We tried to balance two needs in our editing of the units. First, we wanted to maintain the integrity of each teacher's unit. Second, we wanted to be sure to have both consistency (of terminology, of format, of essential philosophy) and variety (in instructional strategies, use of groups, assessment methods, etc.). The teachers who created the units have approved the changes we made or have helped us see how to make necessary modifications more appropriately.

Also, please note that we have opted to make the units somewhat more generic than specific. As teachers, we sometimes have the habit of looking for exact matches for our classroom needs and jettisoning whatever doesn't match. As authors, we can't eliminate the habit, but we wanted to make it a little harder to exercise. For example, although we have taken great care to list state standards reflected in each unit, we have intentionally not listed the name of the state from which the standards came. (It's amazing how similar standards on the same topic are across states.) We're hopeful of making the point that good differentiation is attentive to standards and other curricular requirements, but we want to help readers avoid the inclination to say, "Oh, these aren't *my* standards, so this wouldn't work in my classroom."

Finally, we decided to include solid units rather than "showcase" ones. What's here is more roast beef than Beef Wellington. We wanted to include units that demonstrate coherence, focused instruction, thoughtful engagement of students, and flexibility; we *did not* want to include units that dazzle the imagination. After all, although it may be fascinating to watch someone tap dance on the ceiling, few of us are inclined to try it ourselves. Hopefully, the units in this book are familiar enough to be approachable, but venture far enough into the unfamiliar to provide challenge for future growth. In fact, in this regard, our aim for readers is similar to what we recommend for students: pushing them a little beyond their comfort zones. If all readers feel totally at ease with the units, we've lowered the bar. If we send all readers running, we've set the bar too high. (In the latter instance, some judicious rereading over a period of professional growth just might be worthwhile.)

It may well be that the greatest pleasure of teaching comes from learning. It is our hope that the book as a whole will serve as one catalyst for helping teachers become the very best professionals they can be.

PART I

A Brief Primer on Differentiation

What Is Differentiated Instruction?

Differentiated instruction is really just common sense. Most parents learn pretty quickly that they must differentiate their parenting for children who simply are not identical in the ways they approach life. Perhaps one child in a family is a daredevil, charging at the world and taking physical risks from the earliest opportunities. She needs some parental restraints to help protect her from danger, but she also needs additional opportunities to develop the physical prowess that seems so important to her. A second child is more timid physically and needs encouragement to jump into the pool, ride a bike, or try out for a team. For this child, parents might push a little more in areas where, with their other child (*too* independent and physically confident?), they would hold back. One of the children may need a great deal of sleep, while the other can get by easily with very little. One may like virtually all foods, while the other is a picky eater. From infancy on, one may be content to sit quietly and turn the pages of a book, while

the other shows neither the patience nor the inclination for reading in the early years.

These are just a few of scores of differences children in the same family might exhibit. While effective parents work from a coherent (although not totally static) set of beliefs and principles about parenting, they also learn that their application of these principles will inevitably change as different children demonstrate different needs—and, in fact, as the parents themselves garner more experience in their roles.

In the classroom, the challenges are even greater. One child enters kindergarten reading like a 4th grader. Another comes with no understanding of letters or letter sounds. One child pays attention faithfully when the teacher gives directions. Another child has great difficulty attending to the teacher under almost all circumstances. One child has surprisingly well developed fine-motor skills. Another child struggles with basic gross-motor movements.

Effective teachers, like effective parents, work from a coherent but ever-evolving set of beliefs and principles about teaching and learning. These teachers also understand that how they apply these fundamental principles will vary as they focus on children with different needs and as they themselves become more experienced classroom leaders.

Differentiated teaching is responsive teaching. It stems from a teacher's solid (and growing) understanding of how teaching and learning occur, and it responds to varied learners' needs for more structure or more independence, more practice or greater challenge, a more active or less active approach to learning, and so on. Teachers who differentiate instruction are quite aware of the scope and sequence of curriculum prescribed by their state, district, and school. They are also aware that the students in their classrooms begin each school year spread out along a continuum of understanding and skill. These teachers' goal is to maximize the capacity of each learner by teaching in ways that help all learners bridge gaps in understanding and skill and help each learner grow as much and as quickly as he or she can.

Meet Some 3rd Graders

Thinking about the composition of a classroom clarifies both the need for differentiation and the challenge this kind of responsive teaching presents for a teacher. Let's make the the acquaintance of some 3rd graders, who are about to become a part of Ms. Johnson's group of 26 young learners, ranging in age from 7 to 9.

Iliana speaks little English, but she's learning quickly. Her parents are multilingual and speak English at home as often as possible to help her learn the new language. Iliana likes math computation because the words don't trip her up so badly. Word problems, however, are still a chore.

Tia doesn't speak a lot of English, either. Neither do her parents, who immigrated to a new country looking for better employment. Tia is very quiet in class and speaks only when pushed to do so.

Michael, who is black, is beginning to wonder why he rarely sees people who look like him in the books he reads in class. He also wonders why he's the only black boy in his class who seems to really enjoy math. He likes math best when the teacher asks students to figure out how to solve problems using what they've learned. He works best with classmates rather than alone.

Andrea is very creative and loves talking about ideas. She has a significant learning disability, however, and has a very difficult time with the sequencing required both in math and in reading. She finds reading especially tedious because the books seem silly and simple to her. She thrives on problems that can be solved in a variety of ways.

Sherita is very bright, reading at an 8th grade level. She has broad general knowledge and also thinks in very abstract ways. She rarely learns new things at school, and the days spent waiting to encounter something different and interesting seem very long. She daydreams about horses a lot and likes books on astronomy, when she can find them.

Landry is good with numbers and excellent at art. He has never liked reading, and he has difficulty concentrating when the teacher asks him to work with classmates. His concentration is much better when he works alone.

Max is a cheerful, hard worker, but often doesn't have enough time to finish tasks and to figure out just exactly how things work. He really loves tools and all sorts of machines. He is aware that his classmates find school easier than he does, and he's getting further behind in most of his subjects.

Micah seems frightened of lots of things. He hangs back in class, stays by himself a great deal, seldom speaks up during discussions, and appears quite uncomfortable when his teachers call on him. He is absent a lot, and his work is spotty in quality. It's hard to get a handle on what he understands and can do.

Will has both physical and cognitive handicaps. His curriculum is shaped largely by an individualized education plan (IEP), but he enjoys the company and partnership of the other students in his class, and he's happiest when the teacher arranges things so he is part of student work groups.

Yana has incredible ideas—and an incredibly hard time writing them in an order that makes sense to others. She seems to see things in images rather than words and is often reduced to tears when she is asked to write.

Betsy loves to get answers right in class and to finish her work first. She's happiest when she knows exactly what she must do to be correct. She prefers to work alone and gets testy when right answers and formulas for success elude her. She is competitive and pulls away from situations that suggest she may not be best.

These students are a varied lot, but they are nonetheless typical of the academic diversity in most classrooms—and no more or less diverse in their learning needs than the rest of the 26 students in Ms. Johnson's 3rd grade classroom.

Ms. Johnson has a choice to make about the year ahead. She can try to work around the differences her students bring to school each day and move ahead with a tightly prescribed curriculum and timeline, or she can work consistently to understand the variance in her learners and plan to address those needs as flexibly and effectively as possible. The first approach certainly appears to be the easier way. What, then, would be Ms.

Johnson's rationale for selecting the second approach to teaching?

What Is the Thinking Behind Differentiated Instruction?

Ms. Johnson believes she must balance two factors in her classroom: the needs of her students and the requirements of a curriculum. In her opinion, she is a more effective teacher when she plans and teaches with both factors in the forefront of her thinking. In fact, she is guided by her sensitivity to the connections among four classroom elements: *who* she teaches, *where* she teaches, *what* she teaches, and *how* she teaches (see Figure 1). To Ms. Johnson, the four elements form a tightly interwoven system in which each part profoundly affects and is profoundly affected by the others. If any one of the elements is diminished, learning is diminished as well.

Who She Teaches

With each passing year, Ms. Johnson becomes more aware that there are a variety of factors shaping her students as learners. The students' faces are a reminder that they represent two genders and several cultures. She has come to understand that boys tend to have different learning profiles than girls do, but she also knows there are exceptions to gender-based patterns of learning. She has come to understand that students' cultural backgrounds can profoundly shape both their views of school and the ways they experience school. She realizes that school may be a more comfortable fit for students from the majority culture (whose background is in sync with the ways that schools and classrooms are conducted) than it is for some minority students (whose cultural experiences and expectations differ from the norms of the classroom). Again, however, she has learned that there are

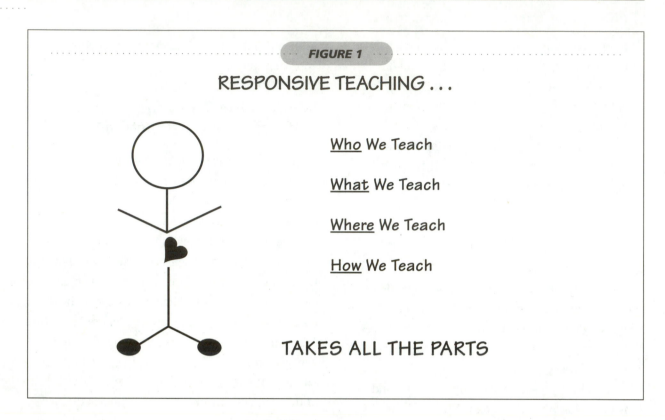

FIGURE 1

RESPONSIVE TEACHING . . .

Who We Teach

What We Teach

Where We Teach

How We Teach

TAKES ALL THE PARTS

variations among the learning patterns of students from each cultural group. Further, gender and culture can combine to affect the "fit" of school for a particular child.

Ms. Johnson also sees a great variety of interests reflected in the faces of her students. They become more animated and involved when the curriculum intersects with their individual and group interests, and she has seen how some of them become excited and engaged by one instructional approach or topic, just as others seem to disengage and float away from her. She knows, too, that her students are shaped as learners by how their brains are structured to support success in a given subject or field. The students' areas of talent and degrees of talent in each area seem as varied as their faces.

Further, due to experiences outside of school, her students do not necessarily encounter school as an even playing field. Some come to school with rich and varied life experiences. Others bring a very limited repertoire of background experiences. This reality, too, causes her students to differ in important ways.

All of these factors—gender, culture, personal interests, ability, experience, and intelligence preference—shape each student to be both like and unlike every other student in the class. Ms. Johnson works to understand and honor both the individuality and commonality represented in her class. Micah, Tia, Betsy, Landry, Max, and all the other young learners enter her classroom daily, dreams in tow, wanting to be optimistic about the learning journey ahead. Ms. Johnson knows that the dreams are not identical and that the learning journeys will both converge and diverge throughout the year.

What She Teaches

Curriculum gives students "legs": the knowledge, understanding, and skills they'll use to move powerfully through life. Ms. Johnson's district provides well-articulated curricula, which represent both the district's best judgment about what 3rd graders should learn and the reality of high-stakes testing. All students are required to take the same standardized test in May. Sherita, of course, could take the test in September and still exceed grade-level expectations. Betsy could, too. Michael and Iliana could exceed expectations in math, although perhaps not in some of the other test sections. But Tia can't yet spell or read at a 1st grade level. Neither can Will. Yana would leap ahead of everyone in writing if only she had some help arranging her ideas. Likewise, Andrea would excel with some assistance, even though her writing struggles and Yana's have different origins. It's also true that key student interests are absent from the mandated assessment. Art (Landry's passion) is not on the test, nor is the astronomy that fascinates Sherita, nor is much of the African American or Hispanic American history that resonates with many of Ms. Johnson's students and their families.

Certainly the district curriculum will be Ms. Johnson's blueprint as she plans units and lessons, but it doesn't seem to be the only tool she needs. She will need to backtrack with some of her students in reading, some in writing, some in math, and some in science. Some of the students are missing critical understandings and skills in all those subjects, but many will need additional instruction in only one. For these students, she has to plan to work both backward (to pick up key pieces) and forward (to challenge and engage). To do less would reinforce existing gaps in their learning and magnify their sense of frustration and futility.

At the same time, some of Ms. Johnson's students have essentially completed the 3rd grade curriculum before the year has even begun. It does not seem adequate to allow these students to stop where the prescribed curriculum stops. So in the common units of study she develops, based on the concepts and understandings reflected in the 3rd grade standards, she will find regular opportunities for some of her students to fill in gaps in knowledge and skill that precede the required curriculum *and* regular opportunities for other students to move beyond the 3rd grade expectations.

Ms. Johnson will also systematically find space in her curriculum to extend the varied interests her students bring to class and to expand their interests as well. She can't really get to know her students' points of entry into learning and then disregard them. In other words, the more fully she understands *who* she teaches, the more aware she is that she must adapt *what* she teaches to serve individual learners well.

Where She Teaches

Ms. Johnson understands that the learning environment she creates in her classroom may be the single most important make-or-break element in helping her students become the best they can be. This is a matter of the heart. In a hundred subtle ways, the learning environment sends each student continual messages about how the class will be. How does the teacher communicate genuine belonging to Tia, who speaks virtually no English, or to Michael, who even at a young age is grappling with issues of race? How does she ensure that Max feels affirmed instead of like he's always running a losing race? How does she help her 3rd graders have real respect for Will, who wants to be one of the group despite the physical and cognitive differences that often seem to isolate him from his peers? How does she convey to Sherita that there is always something new to be learned? How does she help Betsy feel safe enough to risk failure and Micah safe enough to stop hiding?

Tia cannot feel welcome and affirmed in a place where her background seems peripheral to the class agenda or where her current communication limitations make her feel inconvenient. Michael can't feel like school belongs to him if he does not see himself, his parents, and his neighbors reflected in the curriculum. Max and Will can't thrive in a place that continually consigns them to last place in a race to reach benchmarks. Sherita can't feel that she matters if no one cares to provide activities or materials that fit and challenge her. Andrea and Yana cannot find affirmation and use for their rich ideas if they're unable to negotiate the barriers that keep them from writing those ideas down and sharing them with the world.

It is not likely that these students will each find the classroom inviting if there is only one set of benchmarks for success, an inflexible curriculum, or a single timeline for growth. The learning environment in Ms. Johnson's classroom is linked solidly to the varied needs of her students, the ways in which she can work with a curriculum that is both prescribed and pliable, and the ways in which she can enlist each of her learners in developing a place that attends to the needs of individuals as well as the needs of the group.

How She Teaches

Because Ms. Johnson sees and values the individuals in her class, she knows she will need to teach each in accordance with his or her readiness levels, interests, and best modes of learning. Therefore, Ms. Johnson's central goal is a flexible sort of

instruction. She will teach the whole class when that makes sense—and small groups when that makes better sense. She will support students in attaching their own interests to curricular goals. She will provide multiple ways of learning what needs to be learned. She will help students come to understand which approaches work best for them under particular circumstances.

It is this "how we teach" element that we call *differentiated instruction.* This element, however, is intricately bound with a teacher's informed and growing awareness of student profile, clarity about the kind of learning environment that invites engaged learning, and analysis of curricular sequences. Ms. Johnson has accepted two truths about her teaching. First, she will never be able to do everything each child needs on a given day or in a given year. Second, the more diligently she works to know her students and match her instruction to their needs, the more likely it is that the year will be successful for the broad range of learners and the more satisfied she will feel as a professional.

What Are the Hallmarks of a Differentiated Classroom?

Ms. Johnson's differentiated classroom will often appear different from classrooms where the teacher practices one-size-fits-all instruction. The characteristics of her classroom stem from her goals of achieving best-fit and maximum growth for each learner. Here are some of the distinguishing characteristics of effectively differentiated classrooms:

There is a strong link between assessment and instruction. The teacher in a differentiated classroom pre-assesses to find out where students are relative to upcoming knowledge, skill, and understanding. The teacher develops units and lesson plans based on what she learns through pre-assessment and on her accumulating knowledge of her learners. Throughout each unit, the teacher continually assesses student knowledge, understanding, and skill in both formal and informal ways, making ongoing adjustments to instructional plans to ensure progression toward individual and group goals. The teacher also assesses learner interests and learning profiles in order to enhance individual motivation and learning efficiency. Finally, the teacher often provides more than one way for students to show what they know, understand, and can do. The goal of multiple assessment formats is to ensure that students have a way to show what they have accomplished during a sequence of study.

The teacher is clear about learning goals. In effectively differentiated classrooms, the teacher specifies what students should know, understand, and be able to do for each unit of study. This clarity allows the teacher to focus on essential learning goals with all students, but at varying degrees of complexity, with varied support systems, and so on. The teacher also maps sequences of skills and understanding that precede and extend beyond the grade-level curriculum. This enables the teacher to help students make up learning deficits and continue their learning beyond prescribed levels in an organized fashion that can be linked directly to both grade-level goals and individual needs.

The teacher groups students flexibly. At times, the class works as a whole. At times, students work alone. At times, the teacher groups students homogeneously for readiness, based on similar learning needs. At other times, she groups students in mixed-readiness groups, ensuring that tasks call on each student to make a key academic contribution to the success of the group. Likewise, she forms both similar-interest and mixed-interest groups, depending on the nature of the task at hand. She also forms groups in which students have similar learning profiles and groups in which student learning profiles differ. In addition, she sometimes groups students randomly and often guides students in forming their own work groups or making the decision to work alone on a given task. As often as she can, the teacher meets with students one on one to monitor progress, coach them in next steps, and help them set new goals. The goal of flexible grouping is to balance the need to teach students where they are and to provide them with opportunities to interact in meaningful and productive ways with a wide range of peers.

The teacher uses time, space, and materials flexibly. A teacher in an effectively differentiated classroom continues to look for ways to arrange the classroom to enable students to work in a variety of ways, to enable students to use time flexibly, to match materials to learner needs, and to meet with students in varied formats.

The teacher involves her students in understanding the nature of the classroom and in making it work for everyone. When a teacher guides her students in sharing responsibility for a classroom in which the goal is to help everyone receive the support he or she needs to grow academically, the students become a central factor in that classroom's operation. Whether the students are establishing class rules, making suggestions for smooth movement from place to place in the classroom, helping a peer, distributing materials, keeping records of their own goals and progress, or any one of a score of other roles, they contribute significantly both to classroom efficiency and to a sense of community.

The teacher emphasizes individual growth as central to the success of the classroom. In many classrooms, norm-based assessment and grading are the unquestioned rule. In a differentiated classroom, the teacher works consistently with students and parents to help them understand the importance of competing with oneself to achieve one's "personal best." Each student is responsible for working to progress as much as he or she can toward goals that are personally challenging. The teacher is responsible for guiding and supporting that progress. When that progress happens, it is a sign of success. When it does not, it is an indicator that an adjustment must be made— on the part of the teacher, the student, or both.

Parents still want and need indication of a student's standing relative to benchmarks, standards, or grade-level peers. In a differentiated classroom, though, the teacher finds a way to help both students and parents chart personal growth in relation to designated benchmarks. Under any other system, Tia, Andrea, Max, and Will would have virtually no chance for "success" and a high chance of diminishing effort in the face of discouragement. Under any other system, Sherita and Betsy would be rewarded for what they already know without the need to embrace challenge.

The teacher works to ensure that all students have "respectful" work. While students will display different interests, readiness levels, and learning profiles, every student should consistently have work that respects him or her as an individual. In a differentiated classroom, this means each student is asked to focus on the essential knowledge, understanding, and skill that is core to each unit and lesson. Each student is required to think at a high level to complete his or her work. Each student is assigned work that looks as inviting and important as the work of his or her classmates. Drill, practice, and rote repetition do not mark struggling students. Advanced learners are not indicated by tangential tasks.

The teacher makes sure differentiation is always "a way up," never "a way out." It is easy to underestimate the learning potential of any learner. The goal of differentiated tasks is to cause each learner to stretch to complete a task that is difficult but nonetheless achievable, thanks to a support system that helps the learner navigate the unknown portions of the work. A teacher effective with differentiation will always "teach up" to a child rather than teaching down.

The teacher sets her own sights high, just as she asks her students to set their sights high. A teacher effective with differentiation is reflective about her students and her own practice. She is aware of and grateful for lessons that work well for most of her students. She understands and accepts that no teacher can be perfect. She does not accept that she is "doing the best she can." Her goal is not preservation of her current level of practice, but continued extension of that practice through the very last day she remains a teacher. She has a learning orientation and is excited by her own growth, just as she is excited by the growth of her students. She expects from herself no less than she expects of her students—maximum effort to achieve maximum potential.

The teacher seeks specialists' active partnership in her classroom. The effective teacher in a differentiated classroom is much like a good general practitioner in medicine. It is the GP's job to see to the welfare of her patients. She does that with careful attention to each patient's symptoms and needs. Some of the time, the GP can diagnose and treat a patient without assistance; some of the time, she needs to call in a specialist. A teacher effective with differentiation is ready to call on the expertise of specialists whenever a student's needs indicate that would be helpful. Specialists in second language instruction, multicultural education, reading, special education, gifted education, counseling, media, and a range of other areas have focused their careers on developing knowledge and skills often unfamiliar to the general classroom teacher. An effective partnership between a specialist and a classroom teacher does more than benefit individual students; it is also a great vehicle for the classroom teacher and specialists' own professional development, thus bringing exponential benefits to students for years to come.

The teacher's differentiation is largely proactive rather than reactive. The teacher systematically plans for student differences. She does not make a single plan for all learners and hope to "adjust on the spot" if she realizes the plan is not working well for one or a few learners. Good teachers always improvise, of course. But effective differentiation rests upon purposeful planning for student variance, with improvisation as needed.

As this list implies, there is no single "right way" to differentiate instruction. The processes and practices that support responsive teaching vary with teacher expertise, the group of students in question, the time of year, the subject area, age of students, and so on. Effectively differentiated classes are guided by common principles but are crafted in many different ways.

How Does a Teacher Plan for Differentiated Instruction?

By now, it's clear that planning for differentiated instruction must involve careful consideration of student characteristics, curricular elements, and instructional strategies. A teacher at work in a differentiated classroom coordinates these three components with an eye toward increasing student understanding and engagement with the material to be studied. Let's take a closer look at each component.

Student Characteristics

There are three student characteristics that may indicate a need for modifications in curriculum and instruction. These characteristics are *readiness, interest,* and *learning profile.*

Readiness has to do with a student's current preparedness to work with a prescribed set of knowledge, understanding, and skill. If the student can complete a task effortlessly, he or she may make a good grade, but will not learn. If the work is well out of reach of the student's current proficiency, the student has no way to accomplish the task—and frustration, not learning, is the result.

Our best understanding of learning tells us that each of us learns best when a task is a little too difficult for our current level of knowledge, understanding, and skill *and* there is a support system present to help us bridge the gap. In Ms. Johnson's class, for example, Will and Betsy are at very different readiness levels for most tasks within the prescribed curriculum. If Ms. Johnson overlooks differences in student readiness, it's likely that Will will be perpetually confused and will not grow academically in systematic ways. Betsy will receive high marks, but she will not have had to stretch or grow to be an *A* student. Neither will be well served by repeated instruction that overlooks their readiness levels.

Interest is a major motivating factor for learning. A noted artist recently remarked that he never liked reading in school until one teacher asked him to interpret what he read through painting. At that point, he explained, he realized that authors and artists were challenged by the same themes and ideas. He became a better artist for the experience and a more willing reader, too. A wise teacher links required content to student interests in order to hook the learner. Because of the interconnectedness of all knowledge, there are many ways to link what a learner finds intriguing and what he or she is supposed to learn. In addition, effective teachers find "cracks in the schedule" that allow students to pursue their passions beyond the prescribed curriculum. Independent investigations can be effective for this purpose. Finally, the best teachers also help students develop new interests and passions—breathing life and joy into otherwise "flat" curriculum.

Learning profile refers to a student's preferred mode of learning—the way a learner learns best. A student's gender, culture, learning style, intelligence preference, or a combination of those factors may shape learning profile. As we've discussed, some students learn best when they collaborate with peers; some learn best alone. Some students must see the big picture of the thinking behind what they are learning before the parts make any sense; other students work effectively by gathering bits of learning and then constructing meaning. Some students are at their most efficient when they do analytical or "schoolhouse" sorts of tasks; others learn far better when they work on contextual or practical applications of ideas. Some students thrive on individual accolades; others are offended by emphasis on the individual and respond much better to group commendations.

We know many learning profile factors that can impede or aid a student's progress. In a differentiated classroom, a teacher attempts to provide ways of learning that make the learning journey of each student more efficient and effective.

Curricular Elements

There are at least three curricular elements teachers can adapt in response to learner readiness, interest, and learning profile. They are *content, process,* and *products.*

Content refers either to what a student should come to know, understand, and be able to do as the result of a segment of study, or to how the student will gain access to that knowledge, understanding, and skill. As often as possible, teachers hold steady *what* the student will learn and modify how students gain access to the content. For example, all students can work with the concept of community helpers, but the teacher may vary the reading level of materials students study on the topic and may use interviews with community helpers and videos of community helpers as well as readings about community helpers. Occasionally, though, the teacher has to vary *what* the students are learning. For example, perhaps the curriculum calls for students to learn how to tell time. Two students in the class have no concept of numbers. Three students already tell time with accuracy and independence. In this instance, when readiness levels vary so greatly with regard to a basic skill, it makes no sense for the teacher to teach the same content to all the students at the same time.

Process is a synonym for activities. A good activity calls on students to make sense of the knowledge, understanding, and skill specified by the curriculum. Learning has to happen *in* students, not *to* them. Effective activities are focused squarely on the key knowledge, understanding, and skills central to a segment of study and call on students to grapple with the content so they come to "own" it—so they make sense of it for themselves.

Products provide evidence of what a student has come to know, understand, and be able to do over an extended period of learning (generally weeks or months). They call on students to bring together knowledge, understanding, and skill; apply it; and extend it as a demonstration of their power with the content. Products guide students in moving from *consumers of knowledge* to *producers with knowledge*.

Teachers continually assess student readiness, interest, and learning profile, using what they learn to modify content, process, and products to be challenging and satisfying for their learners. A teacher can modify content, processes, and products together or separately in response to readiness, interest, and learning profile.

Instructional Strategies

There are many instructional strategies that are helpful in differentiating instruction. These are strategies that guide the teacher in looking at students in small groups or individually rather than only as a whole class, and they include learning centers, interest centers, learning contracts, mini-workshops, independent investigations, graphic organizers, and collaborative groups.

Figure 2 illustrates Ms. Johnson's planning for differentiation at varied points in the school year as she thinks about her students and uses the student characteristics of readiness, interest, and learning profile; the curricular elements of content, process, and products; and selected instructional strategies to help her match curriculum and instruction to learner need.

Baseball Camp: A Metaphor for Differentiation

John McCarthy, better known as Coach Mac, is director of Home Run Baseball Camp.* Each summer, his work with children mirrors the qualities of an effectively differentiated classroom.

The kids who come to baseball camp at any given time represent as much as an eight-year age span. Their sizes vary. They are male and female. Their past experience with baseball varies. Their talents vary in kind and degree. They represent diverse cultures and economic levels. But they *all* come to camp hoping to get better at their game.

Coach Mac watches the young players carefully, assessing their particular strengths and needs. Sometimes the kids all work on the same drill. Often they work on facets of the game they need to in order to develop most fully as players. They practice individually, in small groups, and as a team. The team gets better as each individual improves.

The coach also sees baseball as an ideal vehicle for teaching the kids about life, and into the drills, practices, and games, he weaves important lessons. He tells them that keeping the equipment ready is the players' job—not his job, not their parents'. Reading is as big a deal as hitting a home run. You can't expect to win if you don't eat well. Shining your shoes carefully says something about your devotion to the game. Coach Mac reckons that in his camp, kids get 50 percent baseball instruction and 50 percent life instruction. He muses that it would be difficult to tell where one ends and the other begins. Coach Mac says neither he nor the kids can control the degree of talent they bring to camp, but each can control the amount of effort they give to developing their talent. "Talent is what you bring," he says. "Effort is what you give." Effort is the great equalizer.

The kids love to compete, love to play the game. "Everyone loves winning," the coach says,

---

*Coach Mac was featured on *The Today Show* (NBC) on August 12, 2001.

·· **FIGURE 2** ··

USING STUDENT TRAITS AND CURRICULAR ELEMENTS TO PLAN DIFFERENTIATION

Student Traits	Teacher Response	Example of . . .
Sherita, Betsy, and several peers are very advanced readers.	For these students, Ms. Johnson includes books with advanced reading levels in most assignments in language arts, science, and social studies.	Differentiation of content based on similar student readiness.
Max loves tools and machines. He has difficulty with vocabulary, spelling, and reading.	Ms. Johnson helps Max develop a growing word bank of tools, machines, and machine parts. They use this as a way of increasing his vocabulary, enhancing his spelling, and prompting his writing.	Differentiation of content and process based on interest and readiness.
Students indicate different interests in the Westward Expansion unit.	Ms. Johnson forms reading clubs based on student interests. She provides access to a variety of books at a range of reading levels for each interest area. Students choose to read books alone or with a reading buddy. Then the interest groups meet to share passages and discuss questions that Ms. Johnson provides and that they generate themselves.	Differentiation of content based on readiness (readability of books), interest (student choice of topics), and learning profile (whether student's preference is to read alone or with a partner). Also focuses on mixed-readiness grouping with supports for successful discussions.
Micah, Tia, Max, Iliana, Will, Andrea, and several other students have difficulty with reading or are auditory learners.	Ms. Johnson (or a volunteer) regularly audiotapes key passages from language arts, science, and social studies so students can listen to the information.	Differentiation of content in response to student readiness and/or learning profile.
Yana is outgoing and has great ideas, but also has serious difficulty with writing. Micah is reticent and struggles to come up with ideas, but is fairly competent as a writer.	For today's writing assignment, Ms. Johnson pairs Yana and Micah. She thinks their strengths and needs might be complementary. She'll watch closely to see how the pairing works.	Differentiation of process based on readiness and learning profile. Emphasis on mixed needs and strengths.

Student Traits	Teacher Response	Example of . . .
Andrea is a good contextual problem solver. Landry is a visual learner. Betsy is a convergent learner who excels in "getting it right."	For today's science activity, Ms. Johnson asks these students to develop a suitable environment for an animal with specific traits. The task calls for research, drawing, and problem solving.	Differentiation of process based on learning profile, with a mixed learning profile group requiring the strengths of all members.
Will, Tia, and Max often need extra support to understand and use key concepts and skills. Two other students have been absent for almost a week.	Ms. Johnson places these students in the same work group for the "suitable animal environment" science activity. She has ensured that the animal traits are straightforward and illustrate key concepts and principles, and she checks in with the group several times throughout the class period to guide and monitor their work.	Differentiation of process based on similar readiness.
Students in the class vary widely in reading and writing readiness.	All students are developing picture books that depict a family during the time of the Westward Expansion. Ms. Johnson gives everyone the option of working alone or with one partner. She has developed project rubrics that reflect goals for all students and goals for individual students.	Differentiation of product based on learning profile (working arrangements) and readiness (rubrics with group and individual goals).
Max, Landry, and several other students have been particularly interested in how the Westward Expansion affected Native American families.	Ms. Johnson encourages these students to focus the picture books they are creating on the experiences of Native American families. She helps the students find books and Internet resources to get accurate information for their books.	Differentiation of product based on student interest and readiness.
Students have varied needs for research, generating ideas, writing, art, proofreading, and editing.	Throughout the picture book development, Ms. Johnson holds mini-workshops on each of the stages students need to progress through in order to succeed in their work. Sometimes she offers the mini-workshops as she observes needs. Sometimes students request them.	Differentiation of product and process based on readiness.

"but winning is a short-term thrill. Long-term satisfaction comes from *success,* not winning." What constitutes success? Giving it all you've got. Getting better. Growing. That's durable.

What do the kids say about the coach? The short players and the tall ones, the pitchers and the outfielders, the experienced and the novice, the talented and the not-so-talented, the white and the brown think he's the best, of course. Why? He really cares about each of the players. He teaches them so much about baseball. When they miss a hit, he doesn't get angry or frustrated, he just helps them learn better. He is their encourager.

There is much in Coach Mac's baseball camp that mirrors the philosophy and practice of an effectively differentiated classroom. He sees and studies the differences in the faces and bodies that stand before him each day. He continually crafts an environment that asks of each person the best he or she can give. What he teaches—the art of the game of baseball—is for everyone. How he teaches, however, varies with individual needs and the needs of the team as a whole.

Neither baseball camp nor school is separate from life. Both are mechanisms for helping young people learn about life as they interact with each other, their coaches and teachers, and the game and content of their curriculum. A primary goal of life, baseball camp, and school is to do the best you can with what you bring. It's the job of the coach—and the teacher—to support that effort.

*   *   *

We hope this primer on differentiation provides you with tools for reflecting on the units of differentiated instruction in Part II of this book—and on practices within your own classroom. Before reading on, pause to consider the following questions:

• In what ways do the explanations of differentiation we provide in this primer mesh with your understanding and practice? In what ways do they differ from your view of responsive teaching? How will you deal with the differences?

• Using the students introduced as examples, augment Figure 2 with other ways you might modify content, process, and products based on student readiness, interest, and learning profile if these students were in your class.

• Think about the baseball camp metaphor for a differentiated classroom. What does the metaphor suggest that's best about your classroom? What elements in your classroom does it cause you to want to rethink? In what ways can you extend the metaphor by adding your own insights to it?

Additional clarification on terms and strategies discussed in this brief primer and used in the units that follow is available in the Glossary, beginning on page 184. To learn more about any of these topics, please consult the Resources on Differentiation and Related Topics, beginning on page 191.

PART II

Differentiated Units of Study

Readers read as they wish, of course, and there's great merit in that. We take away from a source what we are ready to take away, and we gather what we can find in accordance with how we learn best. We would not deny our readers this freedom even if we could. Nonetheless, we offer a few suggestions and questions to guide your learning from the units that follow:

• See if you can find colleagues to read, analyze, and discuss the units with you.

• Read all of the units—or at least several of them—not just ones that seem to address the grade level(s) you teach. Look for similarities and differences. Record what you see. What seem to be the non-negotiables in these units?

• Think about how the unit developers have included and yet moved beyond mandated standards. What's the difference between "covering the standards" and the ways these teachers are *using* standards?

• After you read and study a unit, go back to the list of standards reflected in the unit and the teacher's listing of what students should know,

understand, and be able to do as a result of the unit. Check off those standards and goals you feel the unit addresses effectively. Develop ways to intensify the focus on any goals or standards you feel have not been addressed adequately.

• Look for the links between the learning goals (the standards as well as what students should know, understand, and be able to do) and the individual lessons in each unit. In what ways have these teachers used the learning goals to design the specific steps in the units?

• What benefits for students are likely to occur when a teacher organizes a unit by concepts rather than teaching a list of goals without one or more organizing concepts?

• Think about students you teach. Name them in your head or on paper. Jot down ways in which these specific students might benefit from the differentiated units versus nondifferentiated versions of the same units. Think about students with a range of learning needs, including students who could be described as "typical."

• For which students in your class or classes would you need to make additional adaptations in order to facilitate optimal learning? How might you make these adaptations if you were to revise one of the units? Would it be easier to make the additional modifications in these differentiated units or in nondifferentiated ones?

• How effective do you feel the various units are at

— Beginning with sound curriculum prior to differentiating?

— Making assessment a pervasive and useful element in instruction?

— Providing respectful tasks for all learners?

— "Teaching up"?

— Using flexible grouping?

• How did the teachers who developed these units seem to have decided when to use whole-class instruction and activities and when to differentiate instruction and activities?

• Where in each unit might you incorporate additional ways to differentiate content for particular students in your class or classes? What about additional ways to differentiate process? Products? Which instructional strategies that your students currently enjoy using would you want to integrate into these units?

• Where in each unit might you incorporate additional ways to address student readiness? Interest? Learning profile?

• In what ways do these units call for flexible use of space? Of materials? Of time?

• What classroom guidelines would you want to establish to ensure effective and efficient work in one or more of these units? How would you begin the process of developing a flexible but orderly learning environment in one of these classrooms? How might you enable your students to be your partners in establishing a flexible and differentiated classroom?

• Think about connections between student affect and differentiation as it's reflected in these units. In what ways is the general classroom tone (where you teach) likely to impact student affect? Why? In what ways is the differentiation likely to impact student affect? Why? What connections do you see between student affect and student learning?

• What is the role of the teacher in these differentiated classrooms compared with classrooms in which whole-class instruction predominates? What opportunities do teachers enjoy with flexible teaching that may not be so readily available in more traditional classrooms?

• What portions of your own curriculum do you recognize in these units? In what ways can you build on what you already do in order to address the learning needs of your full range of students?

• Which elements of these units do you particularly like? Which do you question? Talk with colleagues about what you see as positive in the units and what is less positive for you. In each instance, be sure to explore why you feel as you do.

• Try adding your voice to a unit you have on paper, explaining why you have crafted the unit as you have—or why you might now think about modifying the unit in some way.

• Be sure to apply in your classroom what you learn from the units in this book. It's wise to move at a pace and in a sequence that seems manageable to you—but it's important to grow as a teacher!

*   *   *

Our great hope, of course, is that you will be "stretched" by the time you spend with these six units. As educators, we invest our professional lives in the belief that learning is both dignifying and humanizing. We hope this will be your experience in the pages to come.

1

All About the ABCs

A Language Arts Unit on the Alphabet

Unit Developer: Caroline Cunningham Eidson

Introduction

This three- to four-week language arts unit allows students to explore the alphabet through activities based on their individual readiness levels. Throughout, the students are exposed to a variety of alphabet books as they work toward creating their own books. In addition, students are involved in a variety of large- and small-group activities designed to increase their grasp of letter sounds and their ability to apply them. Because it presents information fundamental to literacy, this unit is a good one to use at the start of a school year.

Students in the early grades differ greatly in their literacy skills (some enter school already reading while others may not read for another two years). Accordingly, the differentiation this unit includes is based largely on readiness, with interest and learning profile addressed as appropriate. The first lesson in the unit incorporates a pre-assessment to gauge the students' starting grasp of letters and letter sounds. In addition to participating in lesson-based, whole-group, small-group, and individual activities throughout this unit, students spend time in the ABC Center, a learning center that provides a variety of readiness-based anchor activities that students may complete on their own or with partners.

Teacher Reflection on Designing the Unit

When I designed this unit as the opener for our school year, I knew that I had an interesting but by no means atypical group of students coming my way. I'd already met Dylan, and I knew that he was reading far above grade level. (At the time, I didn't realize just how far above, but it was clear that he definitely knew all of the letter sounds and could use them in both reading and writing.) Salina also had a solid grasp of the letter sounds, and I'd heard she was a quick learner, too. I had also met

Ben, great in math, but in language arts, more typical of a young child than Dylan and Salina. Ben knew three letters—the ones in his name—and he spelled his name "N–E–B." Katie knew a few more than three letters, but I was told that she might have some learning difficulties. Then, of course, there were the rest of the students, each with his or her own abilities, interests, and learning profiles. How was I going to meet all of their needs in language arts but still establish a good starting point for the class as a community?

I began by exploring alphabet books, and I found a wide range of interesting ones that I thought would appeal to students of varying cultures and backgrounds. I realized that while some students might need the concrete approach of the word/picture alphabet books, others might be ready for a more thematic approach. And I figured that all my students would enjoy the challenges presented by alphabet riddle and puzzle books.

Once I had selected alphabet books as my starting point, everything else pretty much fell into place. My job became one of taking an enormous number of possible ABC activities that I had collected over time and matching these with the students who were ready for them and would find them engaging and challenging.

Language Arts Standards Addressed

- Listen responsively to stories and other texts read aloud.
- Ask and answer relevant questions and make contributions in small- or large-group discussions.
- Recognize that print represents spoken language and conveys meaning.
- Know the difference between individual letters and printed words.
- Know the difference between capital and lowercase letters.
- Identify and isolate the initial and final sound of a spoken word.
- Name and identify each letter of the alphabet.
- Understand that written words are composed of letters that represent sounds.
- Learn and apply the letter-sound correspondences of a set of consonants and vowels to begin to read.
- Discuss meanings of words and develop vocabulary through meaningful/concrete experiences.
- Identify words that name persons, places, or things and words that name actions.
- Use prior knowledge to anticipate meaning and make sense of texts.
- Write each letter of the alphabet, both capital and lowercase.
- Dictate messages.
- Generate ideas before writing.

Unit Concepts and Generalizations

Communication

- We communicate in many different ways.
- We communicate all the time.
- We communicate for different reasons.
- The alphabet is one valuable tool for communication.

Unit Objectives

As a result of this unit, the students will *know*

- Capital and lowercase letters.
- Letter sounds.
- Vowels and consonants.

As a result of this unit, the students will *understand that*

- Specific sounds correspond to letters in the alphabet.
- Words are composed of letters.
- Books are made up of parts.
- There are different types of alphabet books.
- The alphabet is important because it gives us a way to communicate.

As a result of this unit, the students will *be able to*

- Identify and apply beginning sounds of words.
- Brainstorm for a variety of ideas.
- Participate in both small- and large-group discussions.
- Make good guesses.
- Work cooperatively.
- Work independently.

Instructional Strategies Used

- Brainstorming
- Learning centers
- Pre-assessment
- Think–Pair–Share
- Independent and group projects
- Learning profile-based activities
- Tiered assignments

Sample Supporting Materials Provided

Sample #	Title	Page
1.1	Suggested Differentiated Activities for the ABC Center	38
1.2	Recommended Alphabet Books	39

Unit Overview

LESSON	WHOLE-CLASS COMPONENTS	DIFFERENTIATED COMPONENTS
LESSON 1 **Introduction** 1 class period	Exploration of ABC books *10 minutes* Discussion of ABC books *15 minutes* Unit pre-assessment *10 minutes* Alphabet sharing and discussion activity *10 minutes*	
LESSON 2 **An Alphabet Riddle Book** 2 class periods	Letter/poem opening activity *5 minutes* Reading and discussion of *What's Inside? The Alphabet Book* *15 minutes* Sharing of *What's Inside* pages and class book assembly *20 minutes*	Creation of *What's Inside* pages based on readiness *30 minutes*
LESSON 3 **Vowels and Consonants** 1 class period	Letter/poem opening activity *5 minutes* Discussion of vowels and consonants *15 minutes* Vowel review and sharing of ABC Center activities *5 minutes*	Small-group vowel/consonant activities based on readiness *20–25 minutes*

LESSON	WHOLE-CLASS COMPONENTS	DIFFERENTIATED COMPONENTS
LESSON 4 **Different Types of ABC Books, Part I** *1 class period*	Letter/poem opening activity *5 minutes*	
	Discussion of word/picture and riddle ABC books *15 minutes*	
	Exploration of other ABC books *10 minutes*	
	Book sharing *10 minutes*	
LESSON 5 **ABC Art Projects** *1 class period*	Letter/poem opening activity *5 minutes*	
	Planning and completion of ABC art projects *30 minutes*	Product choices based on student interest
	Product sharing *10 minutes*	
LESSON 6 **Different Types of ABC Books, Part II** *2–3 class periods*	Letter/poem opening activity *5 minutes*	
	Discussion of thematic ABC books *15 minutes*	
	Think–Pair–Share: Ideas for the class ABC book *5 minutes*	
		Completion of pages for the class ABC book in pairs based on learning preference *40 minutes*
	Class ABC book assembly *10 minutes*	
	Debriefing activity *10 minutes*	

LESSON	WHOLE-CLASS COMPONENTS	DIFFERENTIATED COMPONENTS
LESSON 7 **Lists and Alliteration** *1 class period*	Letter/poem opening activity *5 minutes*	ABC list and alliterative sentences based on readiness *40 minutes*
	List and sentence sharing *5 minutes*	
LESSON 8 **The ABC Book Project** *5 class periods*	Review of the types of ABC books *10 minutes*	Planning and completion of individual ABC books based on interest and readiness *5 class periods*
	Individual ABC book sharing and closing discussion *20 minutes*	

The ABC Center

This learning center serves as an anchor activity throughout the unit and should be stocked with a variety of materials that students can use in different ways to further their learning: magnetic letters, Wicki Sticks (bendable, wax-covered wires available at teacher supply stores), alphabet blocks, alphabet beads and string, alphabet pasta shapes and a pot and a ladle for preparing and serving "alphabet soup," index cards, cards with pictures representing starting and ending sounds, and cards with capital and lowercase letters written on them.

Activities within the ABC Center are differentiated by readiness. Students either choose from an appropriate range of activities or complete specific activities as directed. **Differentiated Activities for the ABC Center** (see Sample 1.1, page 38) provides a list of appropriate tasks. Students who needed further practice with the letter sounds and the alphabet should work on "Level 1" activities, which focus on identifying, ordering, and writing uppercase and lowercase letters and on identifying beginning and ending letter sounds. Students who demonstrate a firm grasp of letters and letters sounds and are ready to begin working with words should use the "Level 2" activities, which focus on creating, writing, and alphabetizing words.

Teacher Reflection on Developing and Using the ABC Center

I find it very difficult to differentiate in a primary classroom without using learning centers like the one featured in this unit. The ABC Center made an excellent anchor activity. Once I introduced these activities to the students, they could work in the ABC Center individually or with partners while I worked with other students in the class.

I decided to differentiate the ABC Center activities because it made little sense to differentiate my class activities so that every child would have to reach slightly beyond his or her current level and then send the students to work on anchor activities that might be much too easy or much too difficult. My solution was to find ways students could use the same materials at different levels of complexity. In this way, I cut down on the number of materials that I had to collect, and I was assured that there would be appropriate Center activities for both the Dylans and the Katies in my classroom.

A few words about the management of this learning center: I did not label the activities as "Level 1" and "Level 2," nor did I find it necessary to color code them (something I typically do with differentiated learning center activities). Instead, I introduced only one or two activities at a time to just those students for whom the activities were appropriate, and I made sure that I was available to give feedback and support as the students first worked with the Center activities. In this way, I could ask a child to do a specific task with a particular material without drawing attention to the fact that the students were working with the materials in different ways. In general, I find that my students are fully aware of who can do what in my classroom, but I do not feel a need to draw unnecessary attention to the differences in the work that they do.

I changed the ABC Center activities during the unit, removing some materials and substituting new activities so that the novelty of the Center would not wear off. Over time, I found that the students naturally began to teach each other alternate ways to use the materials based on what I had shown them. (It was great fun watching the many collaborations that occurred!) By taking time throughout the unit to circulate among all of the students, I was able to monitor their work with the Center activities. I also took time to conference individually with students so that they could share with me the work they were doing in the Center. In terms of record keeping, I kept a calendar page for each student on which I wrote the activities that the students worked on. To make the job a bit easier, I made notes about one half of the class on Mondays and Wednesdays and about the other half on Tuesdays and Thursdays (unless there was something pressing that had to be noted on another day). Over the course of the unit, this format gave me a good picture of how my students were spending their time during both class activities and Center times.

Unit Description and Teacher Commentary

LESSON 1	Introduction	*(1 class period)*

LESSON SEQUENCE AND DESCRIPTION	TEACHER COMMENTARY
Exploration of ABC books. Provide a variety of alphabet books and let the students choose ones to explore either individually or in pairs. This should be an informal activity that gives you a chance to observe the students and listen to their comments as they look through the books.	There are so many alphabet books available (see the **Recommended Alphabet Books** in Sample 1.2, page 39). Throughout this unit, I considered students' interests and readiness levels when deciding which books to use and display in the classroom. I listened to the conversations and made notes when I heard something that told me about what students already knew. (I often use a blank chart on a clipboard with all of my students listed and space for my observations and thoughts.) In addition to being an opportunity for assessment, this activity provided a good, child-centered start to the unit.
Discussion of ABC books. When all of the students have explored at least one of the books, bring the class together for a discussion. Make sure that the students bring their books to share with the group. Good leading questions to ask include • What was your book about? • What was your favorite page in your book? Why? • What is the same about all of these books? • Have you ever seen other books like these? • What is the alphabet? • Do you see the alphabet or letters in our classroom? Where?	I find that my students pick up information by listening to one another during whole-class discussions. In addition, the format gave me another chance to gather information on their readiness levels. I asked open-ended questions and invited students to respond on different levels. I also coached students to build success and extend their learning. For instance, I asked them to identify what they saw in their books for the letter *B*. (I asked about a variety of different letters, making sure to use ones that were in my students' names.) In this way, I invited students to share from their books and to show me whether or not they were familiar with *B* and words related to it. I also asked students to share other words with the letter *B* in them and to tell about other places they had seen the letter *B*.

✳ = Differentiated Component

LESSON SEQUENCE AND DESCRIPTION	TEACHER COMMENTARY
Unit pre-assessment. Ask the students to use paper and pencils, markers, or crayons to show you what they already know about the alphabet and letters.	Here, I got some "hard evidence" of students' understandings that they could keep in their portfolios. (I like to lead students through their portfolios at certain points in the school year to show them how far they've come.) At various point in the school day and while students were working in the ABC Center, I also did quick letter-recognition assessments with individual students to find out both which letters they recognized (both capital and lowercase) and whether or not they knew the sounds that correspond to the letters.
Alphabet sharing and discussion activity. Students share their alphabet work with the class. Ask: Is it important to know the alphabet? Why?	During this discussion, I encouraged the students to share their opinions on the alphabet's importance: "What do we use it for? Why is this important?" This related back to my unit generalization about **communication.**

LESSON 2　　　　**An Alphabet Riddle Book**　　　*(2 class periods)*

LESSON SEQUENCE AND DESCRIPTION	TEACHER COMMENTARY
Lesson preparation: Prior to this and other lessons, write a letter to the class (correspondence) or a poem on a piece of chart paper. Possible topics: The day's schedule, an upcoming assembly or field trip, or an item on the school lunch menu.	Starting each lesson with this activity provided consistency for the students and gave them something to look forward to each day. I used the same letter or poem for two to three days in a row. Doing so not only saved time, it also helped students begin to recognize specific letters and, in some cases, specific words. What's more, this activity was a great way to give the students information about the day—or the week's—schedule and events and to introduce them to poetry. I found that they often enjoyed memorizing the poems!

LESSON SEQUENCE AND DESCRIPTION	TEACHER COMMENTARY
Letter/poem opening activity. Read the letter or the poem to the students, pointing to each word as you say it. Invite the students to read along with you if they'd like.	I used a "magic wand" to point to the letters to add some "sparkle" to this activity.
Ask students to pick out words that begin with specific letters. For example, "Can anyone find a word that starts with the letter *T*?" See how many words the students can find that begin with a specific letter, and underline or circle those words on the chart paper. Ask: Do all of these words begin with the same sound? How do you know?	As we moved through this unit and continued on to others, I differentiated the opening activity by asking students to find words beginning not only with single letters but also with blends and digraphs. Some students were more ready for the challenge than others, but they all benefited from the exposure to blends and digraphs.
Reading and discussion of *What's Inside? The Alphabet Book*. Introduce the students to this book and ask them to share what they think they will see in its pages. Then read through the book, asking students to make guesses along the way about what they think they'll see next. Follow each student contribution by asking, "How do you know?" Note which students can make accurate guesses and which ones struggle with this process.	This ABC riddle book by Satoshi Kitamura introduces a letter on each page and provides clues that invite readers to guess what sorts of objects they'll find on the next page. For example, across the *C* and *D* pages, there are "elephant tracks" leading to the *E* page.
Creation of *What's Inside* pages based on readiness. Following the whole-group work with the book, explain to students that they will be making their own *What's Inside* pages.	This activity was a good extension of the book, allowing students to apply their understanding of how this riddle book "works."
Divide the students into three readiness-based groups, based on their pre-assessment results, and provide each group with slightly different instructions: *Group 1 (Lower Readiness)* Ask students in this group to work with specific letters that they already know and give them help with "clue creation." They will complete one *What's Inside* page. *Group 2 (Higher Readiness)* Students in this group should know a number of letters and their sounds. Allow this group to work more independently, but be sure to monitor their progress. These students will complete two *What's Inside* pages. *Group 3 (Highest Readiness)* Students in this group should already know many letters and letter sounds. Have them either create several *What's Inside* pages or create *What's Inside* booklets, working collaboratively in pairs.	For some students, creating one page provided sufficient challenge. Others needed the "stretch" of completing several pages. While I try to avoid simply giving more work to my more advanced students, here I wanted students who were able to do so to provide clues for their pages, as modeled in the book. By having students in Groups 2 and 3 create more pages (with clues on each page), I was asking them to work at a more complex level. I also asked Group 3 students to work with a classmate to make decisions regarding the objects and clues on each of their pages.

LESSON SEQUENCE AND DESCRIPTION	TEACHER COMMENTARY
	I designed these activities knowing that some students would struggle to work independently while others would be quite ready and eager to do so. Getting young children to work on their own and with others successfully takes a good deal of practice, but for differentiation to work, they must be able to do both. I begin providing practice with these skills during the first week of school, asking students to work independently for just two to three minutes and increasing the time as they are ready. We use the same process with working cooperatively, and practice transitioning between activities so that students learn to move quickly from one activity to the next.
Sharing of *What's Inside* pages and class book assembly. As students finish their work, ask them to share their page(s) with one another in pairs or small groups. When all of the students have completed their pages, put them together to create a *What's Inside* class book—a new addition to the classroom collection of ABC books.	After a few minutes of pair or small-group sharing, I allowed students who had finished their pages to spend some more time looking through *What's Inside? The Alphabet Book* or other alphabet riddle books.

LESSON 3	Vowels and Consonants	*(1 class period)*

LESSON SEQUENCE AND DESCRIPTION	TEACHER COMMENTARY
Letter/poem opening activity. Begin the lesson with this warm-up.	My struggling readers—such as my ESL students and those who had learning difficulties—really benefited from the routine of repeating this activity each day. Pictures and symbols related to the poem provided additional support for these students. This activity also gave me a chance to observe student growth.
Discussion of vowels and consonants. Ask the students what the difference is between vowels and consonants. Write the vowels (*A, E, I, O, U*) on the board. Explain that a vowel can make more sounds than a consonant, and give examples (the *A*-sound is different in "cat" and "cake"). As a group, say the alphabet and stand each time you come to a vowel. Do this as many times as needed.	Another discussion with a kinesthetic element.

LESSON SEQUENCE AND DESCRIPTION	TEACHER COMMENTARY
Small-group vowel/consonant activities based on readiness. The students will break into two groups, who will work simultaneously on different tasks. *Group 1 (Basic Readiness): Vowel/Consonant Worksheet* Students in this group will begin working on a coloring worksheet that requires them to color vowels one color and consonants another to create a final picture. This is similar to a color-by-numbers activity, and examples of this type of worksheet are included in many different phonics workbooks. Allow these students to work in pairs if they want to, and make sure to leave the vowels written on the board so that they can see them. *Group 2 (Higher Readiness): ABC Center Introduction* While Group 1 is working, introduce the higher-readiness group to one or two appropriate ABC Center activities (see Sample 1.1) and allow these students to begin working with these activities with partners. When Group 1 has had enough time to complete the coloring sheets, switch the groups so that the lower-readiness students can get an introduction to one or two Center activities and the more advanced students can work on the vowel/consonant sheet.	Because I differentiated by readiness during the previous lesson, here I asked the students to complete the same work, but I divided them into two groups so that I had a chance to introduce the Center activities to smaller numbers of students in readiness-based groups. I wanted all my students to complete the vowel/consonant sheet so that they could all work on solidifying their grasps of the different letters and because I knew that they would all enjoy seeing the picture that the colors create. I also knew they all would benefit from practicing their fine-motor skills. This activity could also serve as a formal assessment of students' abilities to identify vowels and consonants.
Vowel review and sharing of ABC Center activities. Reassemble the class as a large group to review the vowels, and ask the students to share what they worked on in the ABC Center. During the discussion, invite them to think about the importance of vowels. What would words be like without them? Is it important that they make sounds different from consonants? Why? How do vowels help us communicate?	I led another quick discussion to allow for review and give the students a chance to hear what their classmates had been up to (perhaps sparking some interest in the ABC Center activities). This discussion also let me know what the students were working on in the Center and if they were doing the Center work correctly.

LESSON 4	**Different Types of ABC Books, Part I**	*(1 class period)*

LESSON SEQUENCE AND DESCRIPTION	TEACHER COMMENTARY
Letter/poem opening activity. Begin the lesson with this warm-up.	

LESSON SEQUENCE AND DESCRIPTION	TEACHER COMMENTARY
Discussion of word/picture and riddle ABC books. Tell the students that in a few days they will begin writing their own alphabet books. First, however, they need to spend some more time exploring alphabet books. Show the class a word/picture ABC book, such as *Animal Alphabet* by Bert Kitchen or *Peter Rabbit's ABC* by Beatrix Potter, but don't tell the students what type of ABC book it is. After looking through this book, show the students *What's Inside? The Alphabet Book* again. Ask the students to compare and contrast these two books: How are these books the same? What do they both have? How are these books different? What does one have that the other does not? Which do you like better? Why? Tell the students that these are two different types of ABC books. One is a *word/picture book* while the other is a *riddle book.*	For this lesson and all those remaining, I made sure to provide many copies of different types of ABC books. Here, I presented word/picture books and riddle books, and had the students look at various examples of only these types. This activity introduces a unit understanding. I've found that my lower-readiness students—those still learning the letter sounds—really benefit from the playfulness of riddle books and that my advanced learners—who already know letter sounds—enjoy the challenges riddle books provide in terms of using clues and making inferences.
Exploration of other ABC books. Give the students time to explore other word/picture and riddle ABC books of their choosing. Students may look at books alone or with partners.	I moved among the students and asked them to tell me about their books: "What do you like about this ABC book? What type of ABC book is this? How do you know?" These one-on-one discussions prepared the students for the whole-group discussion to follow.
Book sharing. Conclude the lesson by asking the students to come back together as a large group to talk about the ABC books they looked at. Ask various students to share what type of book they explored: "Is it a word/picture book or a riddle book? How do you know?" Remind the students that they will be creating their own ABC books and that they should be thinking about what type of ABC book they want to work on. Invite the students to share their favorite pictures or pages with their classmates.	I like to give my students as many opportunities as possible to interact with one another and to share their ideas. In this instance, the whole-class sharing format gave me a chance to make sure that the students could identify examples of word/picture books and riddle books and that they understood the differences between the two.

LESSON 5	ABC Art Projects	*(1 class period)*
LESSON SEQUENCE AND DESCRIPTION		TEACHER COMMENTARY

Letter/poem opening activity. Begin the lesson with this warm up.

Planning and completion of ABC art projects. The students will create ABC products using various art materials (alphabet sponges and stencils, magazines, newspapers). Before students begin their work, explain that they can make anything they want (posters, signs, collages), but that before they begin their work, they should think about what they are going to do.	This gave students a chance to pursue their own interests and be creative. Everyone seemed to enjoy this activity (my artistic students especially), and it was interesting to see what individual students did with it. I provided magazines and newspapers so that students who wanted to incorporate whole words into their product could do so while others could focus on using letters only.
Give the students several minutes to think quietly about their projects and then ask students to volunteer ideas that they have.	Sharing project ideas is good way to spark ideas in students who are struggling to come up with an idea of their own. I made sure to call on some reticent students and support their success by asking questions to which they could respond.
As the students finish their products and clean up after themselves, ask them to work in the ABC Center.	Again, using the ABC Center as an anchor activity helped me manage behavior and movement throughout the unit activities.
Product sharing. When all students have finished their products, reconvene as a whole class and allow students to share their products with one another. Post finished products in the classroom for all to see.	My students like to share their work with one another, and I like to see what they've created. Here, I also gained insight into student's developing grasps of letters and words.

LESSON 6	Different Types of ABC Books, Part II	*(2–3 class periods)*
LESSON SEQUENCE AND DESCRIPTION		TEACHER COMMENTARY
Lesson preparation: This lesson features an activity to be completed in mixed pairs, based on learning preference. Prior to the lesson, spend a few minutes creating the pairs, matching a student who likes to write with a student who prefers to draw.	My goal for this pairing was to mix learning profiles with regard to writing and illustrating. I often find that although some of my students do not

LESSON SEQUENCE AND DESCRIPTION	TEACHER COMMENTARY
	like to write, they have great ideas and can show their thinking through drawing. Others genuinely like to write, can express themselves clearly through writing, and would prefer to do that instead of drawing.
Letter/poem opening activity. Begin the lesson with this warm-up.	
Discussion of thematic ABC books. Remind the students that later, they will be creating their own ABC books.	
Ask the students if they can remember the two types of ABC books they have already learned about and explored. Ask them if they can name examples of these two types.	A quick review is always a good idea.
Tell the students that during this lesson, they will look at another type of ABC book and then work on a class project. Read a thematic ABC book such as *Alison's Zinnia* by Anita Lobel or *The Path of the Quiet Elk: A Native American Alphabet Book* by Virginia A. Stroud.	For this lesson, I chose a thematic ABC book that I thought would draw on the interests of as many of my students as possible.
Discuss the book: Is this book an ABC book? Why? How is this book the same as the other types of ABC books we looked at? How is it different? What is this book all about?	I used questions to encourage my students to think on higher levels and to defend their ideas.
Tell the students that this book is an example of a *thematic ABC book*: an ABC book about one type of thing or topic.	
What else could the author have included in this book? How might that have changed the story? How do pictures and words communicate ideas?	My students often like to add their own ideas. I gave them the chance to do so here. This discussion also allowed me to introduce the unit concept of **communication**.
Tell the students that the class is going to create its own thematic ABC book called *The Kindergarten ABC Book*.	A class book was a natural fit for this unit. I have found that my students enjoy making class books, and the more often we do it, the easier it becomes.
Think–Pair–Share: Ideas for the class ABC book. Use Think–Pair–Share to get the students thinking about what might go into the ABC book. Give the students a moment to think about what words could be included in a book about kindergarten. What ideas do we want to communicate?	I used a Think–Pair–Share here because I wanted to focus all the students on the topic at hand, and this approach gives every individual a chance to share an idea with someone else.

LESSON SEQUENCE AND DESCRIPTION	TEACHER COMMENTARY
Ask the students to turn to a partner (someone sitting next to them) and share their ideas with that person.	
Next ask the students to share their ideas with the large group as you write their ideas on the board. What letters do these words begin with?	I wrote the letters *A–Z* on the board so that we could check them off as the students finished their ABC pages.
Completion of pages for the class ABC book in pairs based on learning preference. Arrange the students in the mixed pairs you have created. Tell the pairs that they are going to create pages for the class ABC book, and assign each pair two or three letters to work with. The students will work with their partners to come up with words that match their letters and that tell about what life is like in kindergarten. One student in each pair will write the words and the other student will draw pictures to go along with the words, but both students will participate in deciding what to include on the page.	Again, I was careful to match a student who liked to write with a student who liked to draw.
Class ABC book assembly. As the pairs finish their pages, work as a large group to put the pages in order by spreading them out across the floor or in the hallway. Which page should come first? Second? Third? Next? Staple the pages together along with a title page.	I began this process while the pairs were finishing their work so that those who finished first would not be unoccupied. Of course, students who finished early might also have worked in the ABC Center.
Debriefing activity. Read the finished *The Kindergarten ABC Book* to the class. Ask the students to recall what type of ABC book this is. Which type of ABC book—word/picture, riddle, or thematic—do they like best? Why? Also, discuss what each pair had to do to finish their pages.	As part of the closure for this lesson, I asked the students to think about how well they worked with one another and related the discussion to the concept of **communication**.
Ask: What did you do to finish your work? Did you have to cooperate? How? What did you do well? What could you have done better?	I find that debriefing after small-group or partner work helps my students to cooperate and work together better the next time we do it. These skills are non-negotiables in a differentiated classroom.

LESSON 7   Lists and Alliteration   *(1 class period)*

LESSON SEQUENCE AND DESCRIPTION	TEACHER COMMENTARY
Letter/poem opening activity. Begin the lesson with this warm-up.	

LESSON SEQUENCE AND DESCRIPTION	TEACHER COMMENTARY
ABC list and alliterative sentences based on readiness. Divide the class into two groups based on readiness levels with regard to the alphabet so that one group is made up of advanced students and the other is made up of less-advanced or struggling students. While you work with one group of students, the other group will work in the ABC Center.	This lesson incorporates activities that classes often participate in as whole groups. However, because the activities really address different readiness levels, I decided to match them to the most appropriate learners.
Group 1 (Higher Readiness): Alliterative Sentences Activity These students will work with alliteration. Write an alliterative sentence on the board, have a student in the group read it aloud, and ask the students what they notice about the sentence.	I wanted my higher-readiness students to apply their grasp of letter sounds, and I've found that my students enjoy the word play involved in creating alliterative sentences.
Be sure to accept all answers, but lead students to see that almost all of the words in the sentence begin with the same sound (although not necessarily the same letter).	As often as possible, I let students discover on their own what I want them to see. To that end, I make sure students are clear on the correct answer when there is one.
Explain to the students that the sentence is *alliterative*, and tell them that they will be writing their own alliterative sentences.	Young children love learning big words, so I always give the real terminology.
Begin by choosing the name of a child in the group (for example, John). Have the students brainstorm as many words as they can that begin with the *J*-sound and write their words on the board. Next, read through all of the words, adding new ones as the students come up with them.	I do a lot of brainstorming with my students so they understand the ground rules early in the year: Everyone participates. All answers are OK. None are wrong.
Ask the students to tell you which of the words are things that they can do, and circle these words as they identify them. Tell the students that these words are action words and that we call them *verbs*.	This was my way to get the students thinking about grammar and the special jobs that words can have in a sentence. Again, I gave them the real terminology and pointed out that just as books have different parts or jobs, so do words in a sentence.
Begin the sentence with John doing something, such as "John jumps" or "John juggles." Then ask leading questions so that the students can add to the sentence. For example, "Where is John doing this?" "Who is he doing it with?" "Why?"	
Ask John and the rest of the students in the group to select the options they like best and write their full sentence on the board.	
(*Heads Up!* At this point, it's a good idea to let the Group 2 students who are working in the ABC Center know that they need to finish their work and get ready to work with you.)	I believe in giving warnings so that the students know when their time will be up.

LESSON SEQUENCE AND DESCRIPTION	TEACHER COMMENTARY
Tell the students that they will work in pairs to write their own alliterative sentences. Before they begin their work, review the steps that you went through as a group so that the students know exactly what you expect them to do. Allow Group 1 students to select partners and begin their work. Tell them that after they write an alliterative sentence they may illustrate it. When they finish an alliterative sentence, they may either work on other sentences or in the ABC Center.	Before I sent Group 1 students off to work independently of me, I made sure that they were clear about what they needed to do. I've found that reviewing requirements first cuts down on problem behaviors once students are working without direct teacher supervision.
Group 2 (Lower Readiness): ABC List Activity Explain to this group that they will be working on an "ABC List" and show them the alphabet written vertically on chart paper.	I wanted my lower-readiness students to continue working on establishing their grasp of beginning letter sounds.
Tell the students that together, you are going to make an alphabetized list of things. Ask them to choose between making a list of animals and making a list of foods.	My lower-readiness students tend to need my support more than my higher-readiness students do. For this lesson, they worked with me to create one group list rather than creating lists of their own. Posters and charts depicting animals or foods helped support ESL students through visual cues. I also allowed ESL students to think of examples in their native languages.
When they have chosen a topic, give them a couple of minutes to think of things that fit the topic. Then ask the students to raise their hands to share their ideas by telling which letters their ideas go with. For instance, if the group were working with types of food, "banana" would go with *B*.	
Make sure that all of the students get a chance to contribute to the list, but write down only one idea per letter.	I tried to reserve some letters for specific students so that they could experience success with this activity. For example, I asked a student who only really knew four letter sounds to provide an idea for one of those.
Once the students have come up with ideas for as many of the letters as they can, ask them to create illustrations to go along with the list by selecting a letter and drawing a picture of the food or animal that goes with it.	Creating their illustrations gave the students a chance to work independently and to further their grasp of letter sounds.

LESSON SEQUENCE AND DESCRIPTION	TEACHER COMMENTARY
List and sentence sharing. Bring all of the students together so that they can share their work with the whole group. Allow students in both groups to share what they came up with (sentences or words) and their illustrations. Post the students' work in the classroom.	As I had hoped, this sharing session inspired students (even lower-readiness students) to play with letter sounds and alliteration on their own.

LESSON 8	The ABC Book Project	(5 class periods)

LESSON SEQUENCE AND DESCRIPTION	TEACHER COMMENTARY
Lesson preparation: This is a long project that spans several class periods. It may be helpful to ask for parent volunteers to help you during the course of this project.	
Review of the types of ABC books. Quickly review the three types of ABC books by showing several pages from ABC books and asking the students to tell you what type of ABC books they are. How do they know?	This review also served as a quick assessment of the students' understandings of different types of ABC books.
Planning and completion of individual ABC books based on interest and readiness. Explain to the students that this project is a long one. During it, they will plan their book and then create it. Allow students who need it time to look through the class collection of ABC books to help them decide what they want to do. Others will know what they want to do almost immediately. Ask the students to think about what type of ABC book they would like to make. As they share their ideas with the class, write down their plans so that you can refer back to them to remind the students of what they chose. Prompt them by asking, "What makes a good ABC book?" Using an ABC book that the class is familiar with, ask the students to identify the parts of the book. Ask: How are the pages ordered? What comes first in a book after the cover? Make sure that all of the students can identify the front and back covers of the book and that they can show you the title page inside the front cover.	I wanted to give students an opportunity to pursue their own individual interests. I also knew I could further differentiate the project by varying my expectations for students' work and by encouraging students to tackle different degrees of challenge within the project. For example, I expected (and encouraged) my more advanced learners to incorporate greater depth of thought in their books by using a thematic approach. On the other hand, I did not want to frustrate my struggling learners, so I helped them choose an approach that enabled them to be successful. The majority of my students, just beginning to grasp beginning letter sounds, created a word/picture book.

LESSON SEQUENCE AND DESCRIPTION	TEACHER COMMENTARY
Give each student two pieces of construction paper and show them how they can use them as the front and back covers of their books.	I have also had students create "hard-cover" books using cardboard, wall-paper, and rubber cement. Students sew their pages together, making sure to provide extra pages to glue to the insides of their covers. This is a much more involved way to complete this project, but I've found that it's well worth the effort.
Ask: What is the title of your book? Remind students to think of titles that go along with what their books are about. Would it make sense to call your book a counting book if it is about the alphabet? When the students have finished their book covers, they will create their title pages using copy paper. Ask: Where does the title page go? What is on a title page? As the students finish pieces of their books, clip the pages together or put them in folders so that nothing gets lost. The students will continue their work on this project over several days as they work on their ABC pages. Meet with students individually or in small groups to ensure that they are making progress and that they are sticking to the type of ABC book they initially chose. Some students will need more help with their books than others. As students finish their books, encourage them to work in the ABC Center.	I asked students who needed help with writing to dictate their titles to me as I wrote them on their book covers. While I knew it might be useful to allow some students to work with one another to complete a book, I decided it was best to let each of them make his or her own. Not only did the students get a sense of completion by participating in this project, but it also gave me ample information about their grasp of letter sounds, their understanding of different types of ABC books, their ability to identify parts of a book, and their ability to plan and complete their work. In this way, this project also served as my assessment for the unit.
Individual ABC book sharing and closing discussion. When all of the students have finished their ABC books, give them time to share them with one another. End the unit with a discussion of how the alphabet helps us **communicate**.	At the conclusion of this formal sharing session, we added all the ABC books created to our classroom library so that students could spend additional time exploring them on their own.

Teacher Reflection on the Unit

I've taught this unit several times, and each time it feels tighter and more focused. But one thing that remains the same is my students' high degree of engagement with the unit activities. I think the time that I put into assessing where students are and matching them to activities accordingly really pays off in that each child is then invited to grow as much as he or she can from his or her own starting point. I know that all of my students must know and be able to use the alphabet. I also know that children arrive at these skills at very different times. This unit enables me to respond appropriately to my students' needs at a particular time and in a particular subject area. Plus, the students love ending the unit by making and sharing their own books. They get an enormous sense of accomplishment when they see their finished products.

Caroline Cunningham Eidson has taught elementary and middle school students in Virginia and North Carolina. She can be reached at ceidson@nc.rr.com.

SAMPLE 1.1—Suggested Differentiated Activities for the ABC Center

Level 1 Activities	Level 2 Activities
Use magnetic letters to put letters in ABC order and to identify capital and lowercase letters.	Use magnetic letters to spell words and then write them.
Use pasta letters (all capital) to put letters in ABC order.	Use pasta letters to spell words and then put them in ABC order.
Use Wicki Sticks to make letters, both capital and lowercase.	Use Wicki Sticks to spell words based on picture cards using both capital and lowercase letters.
Use wooden blocks to put letters in ABC order.	
String alphabet beads in ABC order.	String alphabet beads to spell words.
Ladle out letters from a pot of "alphabet soup" (pasta letters in water) and put the letters in alphabetical order.	Ladle out letters from a pot of "alphabet soup" and write words that begin with those letters. Then put the words in alphabetical order.
Ladle out letters from a pot of "alphabet soup" and write or draw pictures to illustrate words that begin with those letters.	Ladle out letters from a pot of "alphabet soup" and create words using those letters.
Play beginning-letter "Concentration" using picture cards and letter cards.	
	Alphabetize words written on index cards. (Increase complexity by having students look at second and third letters as well as first.)
	Create and write alphabetical sentences in which the words are in alphabetical order (for example, "**A B**oy **C**atches **D**olphins.").

SAMPLE 1.2—Recommended Alphabet Books

Word/Picture Books

ABC Americana from the National Gallery of Art by Cynthia Elyce Rubin

ABC Kids by Laura Ellen Williams

Alphabatics by Suse MacDonald

Animal Alphabet by Bert Kitchen

The City ABC Book by Zoran Milich

Pedro, His Perro, and the Alphabet Sombrero by Lynn Rowe Reed

Peter Rabbit's ABC by Beatrix Potter

Riddle Books

Anno's Alphabet by Mitsumasa Anno

Gretchen's ABC by Gretchen Dow Simpson

What's Inside? The Alphabet Book by Satoshi Kitamura

The Z Was Zapped: A Play in Twenty-Six Acts by Chris Van Allsburg

Thematic Books

Alison's Zinnia by Anita Lobel

Ashanti to Zulu: African Traditions by Margaret Musgrove

Autumn: An Alphabet Acrostic by Steven Schnur (also has books for other seasons)

A Book of Letters by Ken Wilson-Max

The Butterfly Alphabet by Kjell B. Sandved

The Cowboy ABC by Chris Demarest

Jambo Means Hello: Swahili Alphabet Book by Muriel L. Feelings

A Jewish Holiday ABC by Malka Drucker

The Path of the Quiet Elk: A Native American Alphabet Book by Virginia A. Stroud

What Pete Ate From A–Z by Maira Kalman

The Wildlife A-B-C: A Nature Alphabet Book by Jan Thornhill

2

What Plants Need

A Science Unit on the Functions of Plant Parts

Unit Developer: Caroline Cunningham Eidson

Introduction

This hands-on, three- to four-week science unit invites students to explore plant growth and survival. During this unit, students ask questions and devise ways to find answers as they discover why plant parts are important. They also observe plant growth to learn about a plant's life cycle. Writing is integrated throughout this unit. In addition to working with scientific process skills, students engage in writing activities that encourage descriptive and clear thinking as well as creativity.

Teacher Reflection on Designing the Unit

Many elementary students enter school knowing *some* information about plants, but few have really worked with plants in a scientific way. They may have some experience with planting gardens or tending to plants in their homes or neighborhoods, or they may have developed an interest in plants by exploring plants in their environments. Also, many preschool and kindergarten classrooms offer experiences with plants. The bottom line is that students come with a range of knowledge and experiences related to plants and with varying degrees of interest in them and in science in general. With this unit, I wanted to provide an opportunity for students to extend their prior knowledge of and experience with plants while they worked with the skills of science. I wanted the students to learn to ask questions, describe things in detail, carry out experiments, and draw conclusions. Because I believe it's important to get students writing early and often, I wanted to integrate opportunities for descriptive and creative writing.

I began the unit with a couple of informal pre-assessment activities to evaluate my students' engagement with the topic of plants in general and their levels of experience with and understanding of plants. I knew that my job throughout this unit would involve matching students and activities appropriately—not only to ensure challenge and success, but also to ensure engagement, either through the focus on plants or through the focus on science skills in general.

Each time I teach this unit, I find a different way to do it that best meets my students' needs. Some groups need or want more practice with the scientific process than other groups. Other groups are intrinsically interested in plants and in discovering more about them. Despite differences in groups and individual students, my non-negotiables remain the same: I want my students to come to see themselves as capable of "doing" science, and I want them to achieve this through a hands-on approach that invites them to exercise their interests.

Science Standards Addressed
- Ask questions about organisms, objects, and events.
- Plan and conduct simple descriptive investigations.
- Construct reasonable explanations and draw conclusions.
- Communicate explanations about investigations.
- Record and compare collected information.
- Observe and describe the parts of plants.
- Observe and record changes in the life cycle of plants.

Unit Concepts and Generalizations
Needs (main concept), Growth, Change, System
- All living things have needs.
- Needs must be met in order for living things to survive, grow, and be healthy.
- Needs can be met in different ways.
- Living things are built so that their needs can be met.
- Plants and animals (including people) have some similar needs.

Unit Objectives
As a result of this unit, the students will *know*
- The names and functions of plant parts: root, stem, leaf, flower, and seed.
- Plant needs: light, water, air, soil, and food.

As a result of this unit, the students will *understand that*
- Plants have needs that must be met in order for them to grow and survive.
- Each plant part has a specific job that helps the plant.
- If one plant part cannot do its job, then the whole plant suffers.
- A plant and its parts change as the plant grows.
- Plants are important to people in many ways.
- Scientists use specific skills in their work.

As a result of this unit, the students will *be able to*
- Identify and describe plant parts.
- Explain the role of each plant part.
- Explain what plants need.
- Ask questions.
- Make observations.
- Describe, compare, and contrast.
- Carry out simple experiments.
- Record changes in the life cycle of a plant.
- Work independently.
- Work cooperatively.
- Show appreciation for plants.

Instructional Strategies Used
- Closure strategies: Alphabet bag, 3–2–1
- Gardner's multiple intelligences
- Interest surveys
- Jigsaw groups
- Learning stations
- Pre-assessment
- Round robin brainstorming
- Small-group investigations
- Student choice concerning groupings
- Tiered assignments

Sample Supporting Materials Provided

Unit Overview

LESSON	WHOLE-CLASS COMPONENTS	DIFFERENTIATED COMPONENTS
LESSON 1 **Pre-Assessment and Introduction** *2 class periods*	"Find Someone Who . . ." plant information scavenger hunt *15–20 minutes*	Struggling students may work in mixed-readiness pairs
	Creation of class plant web, working in pairs, then as a whole group *15–20 minutes*	
		Independent or partner work based on learning profile *25–30 minutes*
	Alphabet bag closure activity *5–10 minutes*	
LESSON 2 **Working Like a Scientist** *1 class period*	Introduction to science skills *10 minutes*	
	Science skill station rotations in mixed-ability groups *20–25 minutes*	Individualized scaffolding provided as necessary
	Discussion of science skills *10 minutes*	
LESSON 3 **Exploring Plant Needs** *5–7 class periods*	Science skills review *5 minutes*	
	Introductory discussion of human and plant **needs** *10 minutes*	
	Small, mixed-readiness group experiments about plant **needs** *30 minutes to set up, then 5–10 minutes during successive periods*	Groups choose a plant need to investigate based on interest
	Jigsaw to share findings from group experiments *15 minutes*	
		Independent or partner tasks based on readiness *30 minutes*

LESSON	WHOLE-CLASS COMPONENTS	DIFFERENTIATED COMPONENTS
	Sharing of work *15 minutes*	
	Alphabet bag closure activity *5 minutes*	
LESSON 4 **Plant Parts and Their Jobs** *4–5 class periods*	Review of plant **needs** *5 minutes*	
	Lesson introduction and plant part interest survey *10–15 minutes*	
	Plant part experiment setup *15 minutes*	
		Small-group research and product assignments based on interest *3–4 class periods*
	Sharing of group products *15 minutes*	
	Experiment and research wrap-up *10 minutes*	
	Alphabet bag closure activity *5 minutes*	
LESSON 5 **Review** *2 class periods*	Round robin brainstorming review in small, mixed-readiness groups *20 minutes*	
	The Magic School Bus Goes to Seed video *35 minutes*	
	3–2–1 closure activity independently or in pairs *20 minutes*	Individualized assistance provided for students who need it
LESSON 6 **Unit Assessment** *2 class periods*	Three assessment tasks *45–50 minutes*	Modifications and scaffolding provided for struggling writers
	Whole-group acrostic activity *15–20 minutes*	

Plant Anchor Activities

During the unit, students should have access to a list of anchor activities that they can work on either individually or with a partner when they have finished their work on the regular lesson activities. The **Suggested Plant Anchor Activities** (see Sample 2.1, page 61) provides a list of appropriate activities that address various interests and learning profiles. The activities encourage students to extend their thinking about plants, and they highlight a variety of learning profiles. For example, there are activities designed for verbal learners, mathematical learners, creative thinkers, and artistic and musical students. Allowing students to choose, or even design, their own activities helps to ensure that they will be engaged with those activities.

Post a list of plant anchor activities in the classroom for all to see, and make sure students have access to the materials they'll need, including a variety of books at multiple reading levels, magazines, catalogs, and outdated floral calendars and date books.

Teacher Reflection on the Use of Anchor Activities

Because this unit involves growing plants and observing that growth (which rarely goes "as scheduled") and because students never seem to finish work at the same time or in the time that I provide, I knew that I needed to approach the issue of time during this unit with flexibility. Anchor activities provide a solution.

Some of my students were able to select and begin activities on their own while others needed some encouragement and guidance. I provided assistance and feedback as I circulated around the room during small-group and individual work times. Also, on Fridays, I always provide time for my students to complete work they have not finished during the week. For those who had finished all of their work, this was a great time to pursue some plant anchor activities. Fridays were also a good time for my students to share their anchor activities with one another.

Unit Description and Teacher Commentary

LESSON 1	Pre-Assessment and Introduction	(2 class periods)
LESSON SEQUENCE AND DESCRIPTION		TEACHER COMMENTARY
"Find Someone Who . . ." plant information scavenger hunt. Begin the unit by giving each student a pencil and four different-colored index cards with the following instructions on the cards:		One challenge of teaching children is finding ways to engage them quickly in a particular unit of study. I chose this activity to get my students involved in the topic of plants and to get them up and moving!

LESSON SEQUENCE AND DESCRIPTION	TEACHER COMMENTARY
• Card 1: Find someone who knows two things that plants need. • Card 2: Find someone who has a garden. • Card 3: Find someone who can name three parts of a plant. • Card 4: Find someone who can name a type of plant. Tell the students that they are to walk quietly around the room to find classmates who fit the instructions on each card. When they find a classmate who fits a card description, they must write that person's name on the card. Each student must collect two names on each card and all the names on all four cards must be different ("For example, you cannot write Janna's name on more than one card.").	I also find that this kind of activity allows students to learn from one another.
Circulate among the students, helping those who need assistance with finding and talking to classmates, with reading the cards, or with writing the names.	Here, moving among the students gave me a chance to listen to their ideas. Typically, I keep a clipboard with me at all times for jotting down quick notes.
In some cases, such as with ESL students or other students who might seriously struggle with the reading and writing involved in this activity, it might be helpful to pair students so that they can help one another find classmates and write names.	In activities like this one, I sometimes put students in mixed-readiness pairs so that struggling learners can participate without too much frustration.
When the students have found two classmates for each of the cards (or when you can see that the activity needs to end because almost all have finished), bring the class together to discuss what the students discovered about one another, asking questions such as, "How many of you found out that someone has a garden?" "Who has a garden?" "Does anyone else have a garden?" Note the students' responses and collect the index cards.	I used the information from this activity (my observations, the discussion, and the cards themselves) to get a baseline "read" of where my students were with regard to their knowledge of and experience with plants. Thus, it also served as a pre-assessment for this unit.
Creation of class plant web, working in pairs, then as a whole group. Next, tell the students that they are going to create a class web about plants and that they will need to share what they already know about plants.	Paired with the scavenger hunt, this whole-group activity gave me a good picture of what my students knew about plants.
Put the students in random pairs and give each pair two paper circles and a pencil. Ask the pairs to work together to write (or draw, if writing is too difficult for some) *one thing about plants* on each circle.	Working in pairs gives students a chance to share and test their ideas before presenting them to the whole group.

LESSON SEQUENCE AND DESCRIPTION	TEACHER COMMENTARY
When each pair has completed its circles, bring the whole group together to share and discuss the ideas while creating the class web.	This was an opportunity to teach the whole class about webbing, and it got the students categorizing and labeling ideas.
Place a larger circle in the middle of a piece of chart paper, and write "plants" in this circle. Ask students to share their ideas one at a time so that the group can discuss them and add to them. As ideas are shared, note when they are similar to other ideas, and place them together around the larger circle, asking, "Does this idea go with any other ideas? How?"	By listening closely and taking notes throughout this activity, I picked up a lot of information about what students knew and understood about plants—and what they misunderstood!
The goal is to begin categorizing the ideas based on the students' thinking and place them in categories around the larger circle.	
Ask: Where might this idea belong on our web? Which ideas does it seem it fit with?	
When all of the pairs' ideas have been shared and placed on the web, invite the students to name the categories: What might they call this group of ideas? Why? Label the categories. Are there other categories still needed? Why?	
When the class web is complete, post it on a wall at the students' eye level so that they can add to it throughout the unit. Tape an envelope holding small circles next to it to allow students to write their new ideas on the circles and tape them with the appropriate category on the web.	I used this web as a visual tool for the whole unit and students enjoyed adding to it as they found out new things.
Independent or partner work based on learning profile. Explain to the students that this new unit is about plants and their needs. Tell them that they have already told you much about what they know about plants and that now they will have a chance to use what they already know to create something about plants on their own.	Here I used yet another pre-assessment (this time incorporating Gardner's multiple intelligences) to help students show me what they knew and to help them learn from one another.
Students will choose one of the following options, and they may work alone or with a partner of their choosing:	Giving students the option of working alone or with a partner is an easy way to incorporate choice.
Option 1: Verbal/Linguistic Intelligence Write a letter to a kindergartner telling as much as you can about plants. What should every child know about plants? What do you like about plants? Why?	These activities enabled me to cover a lot of ground at the start of the unit, and they invited many "teachable moments" as we discussed what the students already knew.

LESSON SEQUENCE AND DESCRIPTION	TEACHER COMMENTARY
Option 2: Visual/Spatial Intelligence Draw pictures of at least three different types of plants. Make sure these plants look very different from one another. Label as many of their parts as you can. *Option 3: Logical/Mathematical Intelligence* On a Venn diagram and using pictures and words, compare and contrast plants and animals. What is the same about them? What is different about them? *Option 4: Intrapersonal Intelligence* You are a plant. What does it feel like to grow? What do you see around you? What do you like about being a plant? What do you not like? Write and draw about your life as a plant. When students have completed their chosen task, invite them to share their products with their classmates.	Most of my students already knew the basics about plants—and those who didn't generally picked them up by the end of this lesson.
Alphabet bag closure activity. Using a bag with each letter of the alphabet included (these can be written on small cards or can be small, manipulative letters), draw a letter out of the bag and ask students to come up with sentences or statements about plants that begin with that letter. (For example, "*A = A* plant needs water." "*D = D*on't forget to water a plant.") Make sure that the students understand this process, as it will be used throughout the unit.	This was a quick way to summarize much of what we had discussed in the lesson. I use this "alphabet bag" approach frequently with my classes.

LESSON 2   **Working Like a Scientist**   *(1 class period)*

LESSON SEQUENCE AND DESCRIPTION	TEACHER COMMENTARY
Lesson preparation: Prior to this lesson, which uses learning stations, write the instructions for each station on chart paper to post around the room, and decide on four "resident experts" who will help the students work successfully at the stations. Make sure that these four students know exactly what should happen at each station, and put one of them in each group of students.	The "resident expert" approach is a great one for helping students to work successfully in small groups. It saves me time in the long run and gives me a chance to move among groups offering guidance as needed. It also gives students a chance to take on some extra responsibility in the classroom. Over time, I give all students—with all readiness levels—an opportunity to be a resident expert; for this activity, however, I selected students who were already reading so that they could read the instructions to their groups.

LESSON SEQUENCE AND DESCRIPTION	TEACHER COMMENTARY
Introduction to science skills. Invite the students to share their ideas about "doing science" and highlight some skills that they already have (for example, writing their names and counting to 20). Ask: What skills do you think scientists need to have? (Observing or seeing carefully, keeping records of what they see, etc.) Record the students' ideas on chart paper so that the class can refer to them during the next lesson.	This was a good place to relate the lesson to the students' interests and abilities.
Science skill station rotations in mixed-ability groups. Tell the students that they will be working at four different stations to practice the skills of science. Then place the students in four mixed-readiness groups based on pre-assessment information and reading proficiency. Remember to put one resident expert in each group. Explain the stations and their locations. The groups will spend about four minutes in each station.	Before I use an activity like this one, I make sure my students have practiced working in small groups (first for short periods of time and then for longer ones) and moving quickly between activities. Time spent practicing these skills really pays off in the long run!
Station 1: Observing Each student will pick an apple out of a basket and look at it closely. The students will put their apples back in the basket and mix them up so that they don't know where their apples are. Then they will try to find their apples. What do they have to do to find their apples?	I was careful to provide apples that were very similar in appearance so that the students had to examine them closely to come up with differences.
Station 2: Classifying Given a collection of different shells, the students will put them into groups. How can they put shells that are alike together? How are the groups different from one another?	I gave the students a wide variety of shells that differed in color, shape, texture, and size. I also provided small boxes for the students to use for their groups of shells.
Station 3: Comparing and Contrasting Given a collection of different rocks, the students will select pairs of rocks and will tell how they are the same and how they are different. Can they find two rocks that are very similar? Can they find two that are very different?	Again, I provided a wide variety of rocks.
Station 4: Asking Questions The students will ask questions about anything they are interested in. What would they like to know about animals? Outer space? Volcanoes? One student (or an assistant or classroom volunteer) will write the group's questions on chart paper.	I made sure that the student writing the questions also got to include his or her own questions. Some adult help here would have been very welcome.

LESSON SEQUENCE AND DESCRIPTION	TEACHER COMMENTARY
As the groups work, move among the stations providing assistance and cues as necessary.	I used this time to ask questions that scaffold some students ("How do you know that's your apple?") and stretch others ("Why is it important to look at things closely? Can you think of jobs in which people need to do this?").
Discussion of science skills. Bring the students back together for a large-group discussion to wrap up the lesson. Ask them to explain what they did at each station. Explain the terms *observe, classify, compare, contrast,* and *question* so that they know what we call the skills they were working on. Ask: When do you think you will need to use these skills as we study plants? Do you think these are important skills to have? Why? Have you ever used these skills before? When? Why? What other skills might we need?	I tried to ask students who I thought would be reluctant to speak up about their station activities (because they had struggled with the activity or because they generally don't like to speak up) to do so here. This ensured their chance to share what they knew. I then focused on more complex questions that asked students to predict when they would use these skills. I also asked questions designed to help the students see that these are skills they already use. My overall goal was to help everyone realize how these skills are useful.

LESSON 3   Exploring Plant Needs   *(5–7 class periods)*

LESSON SEQUENCE AND DESCRIPTION	TEACHER COMMENTARY
Science skills review. Begin by reviewing the science skills you focused on in the previous lesson: observing, classifying, comparing, contrasting, and questioning.	A quick review never hurts. This was a good way to refocus the class.
Introductory discussion of human and plant needs. Explain that today the class will begin looking at what plants **need** to grow and be healthy. Ask: What do *you* need to grow and be healthy? As students share ideas, create a **Needs Comparison Graphic Organizer** (see Sample 2.2, page 62) comparing people's needs to plants' needs. Ask: Do plants need the same things that people need to grow and be healthy? How do we know what plants need? Is there a way to prove it?	Whenever possible, I encourage my students to relate personally to the topic at hand.

LESSON SEQUENCE AND DESCRIPTION	TEACHER COMMENTARY
Encourage students to discuss how to prove what plants **need**. For example, how might we prove that plants need light? Should we give one plant light? Why? How will we know when a plant is not growing or is not healthy? What will it look like?	I wanted the students to devise ways to test plant **needs**. I also wanted them to see that it would be important to grow a healthy plant so that they would have something to compare an *unhealthy* plant to. They were really working with the idea of a "control group" here.
Small, mixed-readiness group experiments about plant needs. Students will work in mixed-readiness groups of four to complete an experiment of their choosing. Every group will follow the same instructions and fill out a **Plant Needs Group Experiment Planning Sheet** (see Sample 2.3, page 63) but they will focus on different plant **needs**. The groups will choose from the following: light, water, air, soil, and fertilizer. Tell the students that each group will be given two plants to work with and a **Plant Needs Group Experiment Observation Sheet** (see Sample 2.4, page 64).	Because the experiment required students to work in small groups for several days, I created the groups based on who I thought would and would not work well together. I did provide some interest-based differentiation in that I asked each group to choose the need that they wanted to investigate. If any needs were "left over," I set those experiments up myself. It was important to me that students worked with something they were interested in, and these experiments did not take too much time to set up.
Post the experiment instructions for all to see:

1. Choose the plant need that you want to prove.
2. Make a list of the materials that you will need to carry out your experiment.
3. Write what you are going to do to show that plants need what you have chosen.
4. Check your experiment plan with your teacher.
5. Collect your materials.
6. Carry out your experiment.
7. Observe your plants for several days.
8. Draw and write about what you see happening to your plants.

Circulate among the groups to make sure that they understand what they are to do. You may have to ask questions, such as "How will you give one plant light and not give it to the other plant?" or "What are some things other than soil that you can try to grow a plant in?" | I gave the groups a checklist of the instructions so that students could check off steps as they completed them. Some groups needed this while others didn't.

I helped some groups choose the materials they would need—notably the groups working with soil and air. I did encourage the fertilizer group to use fertilizer sticks, which are easier and safer than using powdered products.

My role in this activity was to observe the students and step in with help when necessary. Once the experiments were set up and the students were recording their observations on the forms I provided, I met with individuals or small groups who needed review, a new way of learning ideas or skills, or guidance toward more advanced thinking. |

LESSON SEQUENCE AND DESCRIPTION	TEACHER COMMENTARY
Be sure to provide a central location for materials that the students need. It may help to assign one person in each group the job of collecting and returning materials: boxes, plastic bags, potting soil, sand, and fertilizer sticks.	Centralizing materials is always a good idea when you're conducting activities that require lots of supplies.
Allow time during the rest of the class periods devoted to this lesson for students to examine their plants, record what they are seeing (each group member should fill out his or her own observation sheet), and share their findings with the large group. Make sure students are recording their findings on the correct day on their record sheets.	As the students worked to make and record observations, I moved among the groups asking questions ("How are your plants different now? Why do you think they are different?") and giving feedback. My students really enjoyed the independence of this activity, but again, I know it helped that they had had lots of practice working on their own and in groups.
During large-group discussions, ask students to predict plant needs based on the findings so far: Do you think plants need soil? Why? What about fertilizer? Why?	Once the experiments were set up, recording and discussing findings took only a few minutes each day.
Jigsaw to share findings from group experiments. After several days, place the students in mixed-readiness Jigsaw groups to share the findings from their experiments. Make sure that there is at least one student from each original group in the Jigsaw groups so that each possible plant need is represented. What did the various groups find out? How did you find this out?	Regrouping gave all students a chance to share their findings. It also gave them a sense of responsibility for the activity. I circulated, offering assistance as needed.
As a large group, discuss what plants **need**. Are some **needs** more important than others? Why do you think so?	Summarizing as a large group ensured that we covered any information that may have fallen through the cracks during the small-group discussions.
Independent or partner tasks based on readiness. Assign each student to one of three tiered tasks to work on independently or in pairs. Make your readiness determination based on pre-assessment activities, the notes you've taken on the students' in-class performance during the previous lessons, and ongoing assessment of reading and writing skills.	Some students tend to need to work in more concrete ways while others are able to think more abstractly. Here, I used a tiered assignment to address that range of readiness. I'm careful not to assume that ESL students always need to work on a concrete level. Pairing them with other students can allow them to complete a more abstract activity and get help with vocabulary.

LESSON SEQUENCE AND DESCRIPTION	TEACHER COMMENTARY
Task 1 (Struggling Students) You know someone who would like to grow a plant for a plant competition. This person has never grown a plant before. Write a list of everything this person should do to grow a healthy plant that will win the competition.	The first task is the most concrete, designed for students who would benefit from restating the experiment findings. These students may be struggling with the vocabulary of plants and their needs.
Task 2 (On-Target Students) Is there something that plants might need that we did not look at? Write about what that might be, and then write about how you might find out whether or not plants really need it.	This activity is more open-ended and invites some creative thinking as well. Still, the structure is a familiar one, similar to that of the group experiments.
Task 3 (Advanced Students) You have found a plant that is not healthy, and you would like to make it better. Write about how you will find out what it needs and what you will do to make it healthier.	This activity is the most abstract, requiring both analytical and practical thinking. It requires students to apply their understanding of plant needs in determining what might be wrong with the plant in the first place and to consider how they might rule out some possibilities.
Sharing of work. Provide time for the students to share what they've done on their tasks with one another.	This was a chance for me to assess my students' grasp of the needs of plants and to give them an opportunity to share their learning with the class.
Alphabet bag closure activity. Draw another letter (or several) out of the alphabet bag and ask the students to come up with sentences about plants that begin with the letter(s).	I like to use routines for review so that the students know what to expect and are more likely to be successful. I've found that routine is especially important for my struggling learners, who often benefit from knowing what's coming next and what's expected of them in terms of the response format. With the alphabet bag, I sometimes add sentences of my own to make sure we're reviewing the essential ideas.

| LESSON 4 | Plant Parts and Their Jobs | *(4–5 class periods)* |

LESSON SEQUENCE AND DESCRIPTION	TEACHER COMMENTARY
Review of plant needs. Open with a review-focused discussion: What parts of a plant help it meet its **needs**? What plant parts are most important to plants? Why do you think so?	Another quick review. I wanted students' predictions about which plant part is the most important to set up the next activities.
Lesson introduction and plant part interest survey. Explain to the students that the class is going to begin an experiment to look at plant parts and their importance. Tell them that the experiment will continue over several class periods.	I designed this lesson, which combines an experiment and group research, to present a lot of information about plant parts. I also wanted students to apply the science skills (observing, comparing, contrasting) that they practiced earlier in the unit.
Explain that at the same time, they will be working in groups to research a specific plant part that they are interested in. Pass out index cards and ask students to take one, write their name on it, and write down two plant parts that they want to learn more about. List the following options on the board so that students can copy them: *stem, roots, leaves, flowers, seeds.* Explain that you'll be announcing their research group assignment once you've had a chance to take a look at their preferences.	Because I had already differentiated by readiness and learning profile and because I wanted my students to be engaged with their research, I grouped them based on their interests. I asked them to provide their top two choices of plant parts so that I had some flexibility in creating the groups. In every classroom, there are some students who do not work well together because either they don't get along well or because they distract one another. I wanted to create groups of students who had similar interests *and* would be productive.
Plant part experiment setup. Kick off the experiment by leading a whole-class examination of the parts of pansies. Give small, random groups of four students one pansy and ask them to find the stem, the leaves, and the flowers. Where are the roots? Where are the seeds?	
Now take back each of the pansies and tell the students that you are going to remove one part from each pansy, leaving one pansy whole. Pause to ask them why they think you're leaving one pansy whole: What will we learn by doing this? What do you think will happen if I remove all of the leaves on a pansy? What if I remove the roots? How is the work we are doing like the work a scientist does?	Again, I wanted my students to make some predictions. I was hoping they would know the answer to this after our previous work with plant needs!

LESSON SEQUENCE AND DESCRIPTION	TEACHER COMMENTARY
Carefully cut away parts (roots, stem, leaves, flowers) and replant and water each pansy, asking students to suggest reasons *why* you're watering the plants. Be sure to label each pansy to show what part it is missing.	
Ask: Will all of the plants live and grow? Why do you think so? Which plants will live the longest? Why?	
The students will observe a pansy of their choice for several days and record what they notice on the **Plant Part Experiment Observation Sheet** (see Sample 2.5, page 65).	It's important for students to have a way to show their observations. Here, I set up a simple chart to provide the structure that young children often need.
Small-group research and product assignments based on interest. Put the students into the small, interest-based, mixed-readiness groups you created. There should be no more than four students in each group; you may need to create more than one small group per plant part, depending on the interest information you find in the students' surveys.	As mentioned previously, I grouped the students based on their interests rather than on readiness or learning profile.
Tell the students that sometimes, scientists must be detectives. For the upcoming activity, they will be detectives seeking information about plant parts. Their job will be to teach their classmates what they learn.	
Provide several books about plants and their parts (see Sample 2.6 on page 66 for some suggestions), and make sure to audiotape some of the books for students who are not yet able to read for information.	I made sure to provide books on different reading levels. Providing books on tape ensured that struggling readers and auditory learners could participate fully in the activity.
Explain to the students that they must work together to complete their research and that all group members will be responsible for contributing to four product assignments. List the following directions for all to see:	I encouraged the groups to do their research (reading and listening) together so that they could discuss what they were learning.
Product 1 Make a small poster of different examples of your plant part. You may either draw pictures yourself or cut examples from magazines and catalogs.	I designed these product assignments to draw on different skills, so that each group member could make a valuable contribution to the group's work. I knew that I wanted all of the groups to create a written product (the letter), and I wanted to make
Product 2 Create a list of the great things about your plant part. Include at least three ideas on your list.	sure the other products called for skills other than writing. Accordingly,

LESSON SEQUENCE AND DESCRIPTION	TEACHER COMMENTARY
Product 3 How does your plant part help the plant meet its needs? List two ways that it works to help the plant. *Product 4* As a group, write a thank-you letter from a plant to your plant part. What would a plant say to your plant part to show it is glad to have it?	the poster draws on creative and visual skills and the lists draw on thinking skills (pulling together all the information learned) without relying too heavily on verbal (writing) skills. Although I encouraged group members to work together to create the products, I did notice that students were drawn to particular ones based on their learning profiles and abilities.
Sharing of group products. When the research groups have completed their products, provide time for them to share the products with the whole class.	
Experiment and research wrap-up. Conclude the plant part experiment by examining the pansies. What has happened to each pansy without specific parts? Which plants are healthy? Which ones are not? Why? Do students think the same things would happen if the class did this experiment again? Why? Why might scientists repeat an experiment?	During this large-group discussion, I wanted to ensure that my students understood what had happened during the experiment. I also wanted to make sure that many different students could respond during the discussion. Thus, I asked questions ranging from ones that focused on the students' observations to ones that asked them to consider what might happen if we repeated the experiment.
Remind the students that they have learned a lot about plant parts from the different research groups and by observing the changes in the pansies. Now, ask them to vote on which plant part they believe is the *most important* to a plant.	My students like to vote and give their opinions about a wide range of topics. Here, I gave them chance to do so . . . and to practice evaluative thinking.
Turn the discussion to what would happen to plants if they had no flowers. Make sure that the students understand that flowers make seeds and plants would die out without them. Ask: What would happen to a plant if one part could not do its job? What can you compare that to?	I took time to discuss flowers explicitly because my students sometimes have a hard time understanding why flowers are important to plant survival.
Lead students to see that plant parts must all work together to help the plant survive and be healthy, and help them see how this might work in their own lives (for example, people work together at home and in school to help one another, the home, and school).	I presented examples here to help students make a personal connection to what they were learning.

LESSON SEQUENCE AND DESCRIPTION	TEACHER COMMENTARY
Alphabet bag closure activity. Repeat the alphabet bag activity, encouraging students to create sentences about plant parts.	

LESSON 5	Review	*(2 class periods)*

LESSON SEQUENCE AND DESCRIPTION	TEACHER COMMENTARY
Round robin brainstorming review in small, mixed-readiness groups. Begin with a review of what the students learned during the previous lesson. Write each plant part (stem, roots, leaves, flowers, seeds) on a separate piece of chart paper and post the chart paper around the room.	Round robin activities get students up and moving and allow them to learn from one another. I used this one to give the students a chance to recall what they had learned about plant parts.
Place the students in five mixed-readiness groups, making sure that each group has at least one member from each of the plant part research groups.	Having each research group represented in the round robin groups ensured that at least one student in each group had a deep understanding of each of the plant parts.
Ask the groups to choose a recorder (a person who will do the writing for the group) and give each recorder a different color marker. Tell the groups that they are to write what they know about the plant parts on chart paper.	Choosing a recorder up-front ensured that the groups didn't spend time arguing about who would write at each piece of chart paper. Some groups opted to have two recorders who took turns.
The groups begin at different pieces of chart paper posted around the room and rotate so that they visit each piece one time. When they come to a paper that already has ideas, they should read the ideas that are there and add to them. The groups spend about three minutes at each "station."	As with all round robin activities, I kept the rotations quick so that the students didn't have time to get off task.
When all of the groups have brainstormed ideas about all of the plant parts, review the students' ideas as a whole group and add to the chart paper as needed: "Is there anything else we need to add about seeds? What about roots?" Point out the connections between the different parts.	Here, we checked and revised ideas as needed. I didn't want my students to have any misunderstandings at this point in the unit.
***The Magic School Bus Goes to Seed* video.** Show Scholastic's *The Magic School Bus Goes to Seed.* Explain to the students that some of the information in the video will not be new to them.	My students enjoy the Magic School Bus videos, which are filled with good information. Plus, many of my visual learners pick up information effectively from videos.

LESSON SEQUENCE AND DESCRIPTION	TEACHER COMMENTARY
Encourage them to listen closely for new information, and tell them that they will have an assignment to do after the video is over.	I warned students that an assignment was coming to encourage them to focus on the information in the video.
3–2–1 closure activity independently or in pairs. Use this activity to summarize the video. Write the following on the board and go over it with the students before they begin their work: Tell me . . . • Three new ideas you got from the video. • Two things you already knew. • One thing you can do to meet the needs of plants. Allow the students who wish to complete the activity with a partner to do so. When the students have finished their work, ask for volunteers to share their ideas.	3–2–1 is a quick way to summarize just about any information. It worked well here as an assessment of student understanding. Working in pairs can result in better ideas, but I let my students choose whether they wanted to work with someone else or not. In an activity like this, I sometimes pair struggling writers with students who are able to write, but when I do so, I'm careful to ensure that both students are sharing their ideas. As the students worked, I offered assistance to those who needed it.

LESSON 6	**Unit Assessment**	*(2 class periods)*

LESSON SEQUENCE AND DESCRIPTION	TEACHER COMMENTARY
Three assessment tasks. Explain to the students that this activity is made up of three parts and that they are to work on each part alone (without help from others). Provide each student with the three tasks: *Task 1* Using a diagram of a plant (this should be included on the sheet), label each plant part. *Task 2* Imagine you are a plant part. Write a letter to another plant part telling it why you are more important than it is.	Although I did not tell my students that they were being "tested," I did encourage them to show me what they knew about plants. The first task is a simple recall that I felt certain my students could complete successfully. The second task asks students to apply their understanding of plant parts and their roles while having to use evaluative thinking.

LESSON SEQUENCE AND DESCRIPTION	TEACHER COMMENTARY
Task 3 Pretend that you are going to plant a garden at school. What will you need to plant your garden and take care of it? How can you make sure that your plants will be healthy? Make a list of everything that you will need to do.	The third task also invites application, but here, students have to focus on the needs of plants.
Allow the students to spread out around the room so that they have ample space to work and think quietly. They may complete the three parts in any order they wish. As they finish, encourage them to work quietly on the plant anchor activities.	Combined, these three tasks addressed my unit objectives and gave me a good indication of how well my students had mastered them.
Provide scaffolding for selected students, as necessary.	To help my struggling writers complete the assessment successfully, I provided a sheet listing the names of the plant parts we'd covered and a template for a letter. Students who needed this assistance could simply copy the plant part names onto the diagram and the letter template. I also allowed them to draw in response to Task 3. With these modifications, they could show me what they had come to understand about plants without being penalized for weaknesses that had little to do with my unit objectives. I also met with individuals or small groups who needed assistance completing the task.
Whole-group acrostic activity. After all of the students have finished the unit assessment, bring the whole group together for unit closure activity: creating an acrostic using the words "PLANT NEEDS." The students come up with words and phrases that draw on what they have learned about plants and their needs. If they would like to, they can also create a "PLANT PARTS" acrostic. Post the acrostic(s) in the classroom.	This activity provided a final opportunity for the students to work together and share ideas during this unit. It was a quick and easy way to end our study of plants and plant needs.

Teacher Reflection on the Unit

Teaching this unit is always great fun. The hands-on activities give my students a chance to really work as scientists. Even when things don't go as planned (such as when a plant lives or dies when it "shouldn't"), my students learn about "doing science." An added bonus of focusing on science is that young children are really natural scientists, and even my most struggling learners can participate in unit activities—and grow from having done so. I've found that by giving the students a say in what they will learn about, I can improve the chances that each of them will participate in and benefit from the unit activities. The closure activities give me a sense of who's getting it and who's still working on developing understanding. This unit helps me deal with the reality that my students bring a range of prior knowledge and experience to the classroom.

───────────────────────

Caroline Cunningham Eidson has taught elementary and middle school students in Virginia and North Carolina. She can be reached at ceidson@nc.rr.com.

SAMPLE 2.1—Suggested Plant Anchor Activities

- Make an ABC list of plants. Use books in the classroom to find the names of plants that begin with each letter of the alphabet.

- Create a collage of plants or flowers. Label the plants and flowers if you know their names.

- Draw and label plants that we can eat. Which do you like to eat?

- Draw and label plants that we cannot eat. Why can't we eat these?

- Design a garden. How big will your garden be? What will you put in it? Why?

- Create riddles or jokes about plants and their parts. Try them out on your classmates.

- Measure the plants in the classroom, and make a graph showing their heights. Which is the tallest plant? Which is the shortest one? Do you think that will change? Why?

- Write a song about plants, what you like about them, and why they are important.

- Design a new kind of plant or flower. What is special about it? How is it different from other plants or flowers?

- Bring in a collection of leaves from home and make a booklet of leaf rubbings. Label the types of leaves if you know them, and look up and label any types that you don't know.

- Make up your own plant activity and ask your teacher if it's okay to do it!

SAMPLE 2.2—Needs Comparison Graphic Organizer

What We Need to Be Healthy	What Plants Need to Be Healthy

SAMPLE 2.3—Plant Needs Group Experiment Planning Sheet

Group members _____

We are going to prove that plants need _____ .

These are the materials that we need for our experiment:

This is what we are going to do to prove that plants need _____ :

1.

2.

3.

4.

5.

This is what we think is going to happen to our plants:

This is what did happen to our plants:

Conclusion: Do plants need _____ ?   (Circle one)   YES   NO

SAMPLE 2.4—Plant Needs Group Experiment Observation Sheet

Group Members _____

Do Plants Need _____?

Directions: Each day, draw and write about what your plant looks like and how it has changed. What do you think is causing the changes?

Day 1	Day 2	Day 3	Day 4	Day 5
Drawing:	Drawing:	Drawing:	Drawing:	Drawing:
Observations:	Observations:	Observations:	Observations:	Observations:
Possible Causes:	Possible Causes:	Possible Causes:	Possible Causes:	Possible Causes:

SAMPLE 2.5—Plant Part Experiment Observation Sheet

The plant I am observing has no (check one box)

❑ Stem   ❑ Leaves   ❑ Flowers   ❑ Roots

Directions: Every day, draw and write about what your plant looks like and how it has changed. What do you think is causing the changes?

Day 1	Day 2	Day 3	Day 4	Day 5
Drawing:	Drawing:	Drawing:	Drawing:	Drawing:
Observations:	Observations:	Observations:	Observations:	Observations:
Possible Causes:	Possible Causes:	Possible Causes:	Possible Causes:	Possible Causes:

SAMPLE 2.6—Recommended Books About Plants

All About Seeds by Susan Kuchalla

The Carrot Seed by Ruth Krauss

A First Look at Leaves by Millicent Selsam and Joyce Hunt

A Flower Grows by Ken Robbins

From Seed to Plant by Gail Gibbons

From Seed to Sunflower by Gerald Legg

How a Seed Grows by Helene J. Jordan

I Wonder Why Trees Have Leaves, and Other Questions About Plants by Andrew Charman

The Magic School Bus Plants Seeds: A Book About How Living Things Grow by Joanna Cole

Plants That Never Ever Bloom by Ruth Heller

The Reason for a Flower by Ruth Heller

Roots Are Food Finders by Franklyn Branley

A Seed Grows: My First Look at a Plant's Life Cycle by Pamela Hickman and Heather Collins

Seeds, Pop, Stick, Glide by Patricia Lauber

Stems by Gail Saunders-Smith

The Tiny Seed by Eric Carle

What Is a Plant? by Bobbie Kalman

Your First Garden Book by Marc Brown

3

We're All in It Together

A Social Studies Unit on Needs, Wants, and Community Helpers

Unit Developer: Jennifer Ann Bonnett

Introduction

This three- to four-week social studies unit opens with a review of the basics about what a community is and then, through a variety of hands-on activities, delves into the concept of **interdependence** within a community. It helps students to develop an understanding of people's interactions within a community, their community responsibilities, and the ways in which they help others in a community.

After a brief look at what students already understand about a community, they move to discovering the importance of each person's role within a community and begin to role-play and explain **interdependence.** Skills emphasized include writing persuasively and using community resources. Through a learning contract related to communities, students practice newly acquired skills, use community terminology, and apply unit concepts in ways that match their interests and learning styles. Some literature is used as supplements to the lessons. Other selections can be substituted easily for the ones cited.

Teacher Reflection on Designing the Unit

With this unit, I wanted to build on my students' existing knowledge about communities and about the town in which they live. I knew that most of my students could tell me where to find the best pizza in town or where to watch a college basketball game; however, they seemed to lack an understanding of how important *people* are to a community and the ways in which people can work together to meet a community's needs and wants. My goal was to create a unit that focused on the curriculum goals while acquainting my students with their town's resources. I realized that I could accomplish this in several ways. I decided to incorporate tiered assignments, cooperative learning, multiple intelligences, and (because writing is a focus in my curriculum) differentiated writing assignments.

Social Studies Standards Addressed

- Distinguish between needs and wants.
- Distinguish between goods produced and services provided in a community.
- Describe similarities and differences.
- Identify roles people perform within their families and their communities.

Unit Concepts and Generalizations

Interdependence (main concept), Goods and Services, Resources, Needs and Wants, System

- Interdependence requires more than one role to be present.
- With interdependence, each role is important.
- In an interdependent system, failure of a role to function properly impacts all other roles.

Unit Objectives

As a result of this unit, the students will *know*

- Places within a community.
- Roles within a community.
- Community vocabulary including *role, need, want, goods, services, products, business,* and *resources.*

As a result of this unit, the students will *understand that*

- People have needs and wants that are met by the different roles within a community.
- Different roles provide for a community in different ways.
- Each role is important to the functioning of a community.
- Without certain roles, a community may suffer.
- All people in a community are part of a system in which a change in one part can impact other parts.
- All people have a responsibility to cooperate in order for a community to run effectively.

As a result of this unit, the students will *be able to*

- Explain the different components of a community.
- Compare, contrast, and evaluate community roles.

- Draw conclusions.
- Work cooperatively.
- Work independently.
- Write a letter.
- Write a set of directions.
- Use a telephone book.
- Analyze a problem.
- Identify and describe one's own role in a community.
- Write and/or speak persuasively.
- Role-play.

Instructional Strategies Used

- Differentiated writing prompts
- Learning contracts differentiated by readiness
- Simulations
- Think–Pair–Share

- Gardner's multiple intelligences
- RAFT activity options
- Sternberg's triarchic intelligences
- Tiered assignments

Sample Supporting Materials Provided

Sample #	Title	Page
3.1	Differentiated Community Learning Contracts	87
3.2	Community Helper Cause-and-Effect Graphic Organizer	93
3.3	Community RAFT Activity Options	94

Unit Overview

LESSON	WHOLE-CLASS COMPONENTS	DIFFERENTIATED COMPONENTS
LESSON 1 **Introduction** *1 class period*	Whole-group examination of community pictures *10 minutes* Community pictures pre-assessment activity in small, mixed-readiness groups *15 minutes* Concluding discussion *10 minutes*	

LESSON	WHOLE-CLASS COMPONENTS	DIFFERENTIATED COMPONENTS
LESSON 2 **Who? What? Where?** *1 class period*	Thinking map activity in mixed-readiness (random) groups *25 minutes*	
	Concluding discussion *10 minutes*	
LESSON 3 **Needs, Wants, and Unequal Resources** *3–4 class periods*	Needs simulation activity in mixed-readiness (random) groups *20 minutes*	
	Discussion of needs simulation activity *10 minutes*	
		Tiered writing prompts based on readiness *20 minutes*
	Sharing of written responses and discussion of needs versus wants *15 minutes*	
		Independent or partner work on tasks based on Sternberg's triarchic intelligences *1–2 class periods*
	Product sharing and closure activity *15 minutes*	
LESSON 4 *Roxaboxen* *1–2 class periods*	Review of needs and wants and introduction of community resources *10 minutes*	
	Reading and discussion of *Roxaboxen* *20 minutes*	
		Tiered activities based on readiness *30 minutes*
	Product sharing and related discussion in small, mixed-readiness groups *15 minutes*	

LESSON	WHOLE-CLASS COMPONENTS	DIFFERENTIATED COMPONENTS
LESSON 5 **Interviewing a Community Helper** *5–6 class periods*	Think–Pair–Share: Community helpers *10 minutes*	
		Interview tasks based on readiness and learning profile *1–2 class periods*
		Products from interviews based on Gardner's multiple intelligences *1–2 class periods*
	Product sharing and discussion *15 minutes*	
		Tiered writing prompts based on writing and thinking skills readiness *30 minutes*
	Sharing and discussion of written responses *20 minutes*	
LESSON 6 **A Kinesthetic Simulation** *1 class period*	Interdependence simulation activity *20–25 minutes*	
		Pair work on cause and effect based on student choice *15–20 minutes*
	Discussion of unit generalizations *5 minutes*	
LESSON 7 **Concluding Activity** *1 class period*		Independent completion of RAFT activities based on learning profile and Gardner's multiple intelligences *45–50 minutes*
LESSON 8 **Unit Assessment** *1 class period*	Independent completion of unit final assessment questions *45–50 minutes*	Modifications made as needed for struggling learners

Community Learning Contracts

Prior to beginning the unit, introduce the appropriate form of this unit's ongoing component, the **Differentiated Community Learning Contract** (Sample 3.1, beginning on page 87), to small groups of students based on readiness. Learning contracts allow students to learn terms, concepts, and skills at their own pace—and for this reason, they're a valuable tool in a differentiated classroom. Learning contracts are also a great way to manage time, as they work well as anchor activities: meaningful and engaging tasks students can turn to when they finish their regular lesson work "early" or during independent work times when they are wondering what to do. When students have work that engages them, their teacher is free to coach students individually and in small groups as needed.

The learning contracts in this unit are differentiated by readiness and color-coded accordingly. The first contract (RED) is designed for students who are working at a basic level and need practice with the unit's terminology and skills. These may be students who struggle with language (English language learners or students with learning disabilities in the area of language) or who struggle with producing work independently. The RED contract is also easily adapted to address the IEP goals of students with learning challenges. It may be necessary to meet individually with these students to guide their contract work and to enlist the help of special educators.

The second contract (BLUE) is designed for students who have a good grasp of the unit's main terms, concepts, and skills and are ready to work with them at a more challenging level. These students think at high levels and generally work well independently. If you have students who are advanced in knowledge but not yet skilled at working independently, you can support their independence by presenting parts of the BLUE contract one at a time, using a timeline with frequent check-in dates, enlisting the support of parents, and helping students set and monitor daily contract goals.

Teacher Reflection on Managing Students' Work with Learning Contracts

I introduce students to the appropriate form of the Differentiated Community Learning Contract when they are engaged in quiet independent work. I simply pull groups aside for a quick discussion—a process I find much easier (and vastly more effective) than trying to explain both contracts to the whole group.

I use learning contracts frequently in my classroom because they help me manage time, and they are an effective way to respond to my students' varying needs. I also find that contracts can be a good way to inject some creativity into my students' day. Often, I must spend so much time making sure that my students have the basics that it's nice to have the chance to give them something a little bit more open and original. The most difficult part of using contracts comes at the start: finding and selecting or creating activities that will engage my students' interests and give them a good, but "doable," challenge. I've learned that if I plan the contract activities correctly, my students find them engaging, and after some initial practice with working independently, behavior is rarely a problem.

I allow students to work on their contract activities with others when I know that doing so will invite success for them. Some of my students can and should work on their own, while others really benefit from the input and assistance of others. When students do work in pairs, I establish with them from the very beginning (and revisit as needed) that both students must contribute to the completion of the contract tasks. Again, if I've thought out my student pairings well, this isn't usually an issue.

Once my students begin working on their contracts, my job is really all about observing them, providing feedback and assistance when they need it, and coaching each student for highest quality work. I can also use some of the times when students are working on their contracts to teach small groups of students based on common needs. I find that moving among the students as they work gives me multiple opportunities to interact with them personally about their work, to probe their thinking, and to stretch them a bit further than they might go without some prodding. I provide checklists to those who need the structure of checking tasks off as they complete them, and I encourage everyone to set goals along the way. I also invite students to share their contract products with one another both informally as they finish them and formally at set times during our week. When they share their work, I ask the class to provide helpful feedback and to identify strengths. I also ask students to consider what they like about their *own* work, what they might change about it, and how they would do it differently in the future.

Unit Description and Teacher Commentary

LESSON 1	Introduction	(1 class period)

LESSON SEQUENCE AND DESCRIPTION	TEACHER COMMENTARY
Whole-group examination of community pictures. Begin the lesson by showing pictures of communities from around the world. (Use social studies texts, magazines, photographs, etc.) Kick off the discussion by focusing on what the students notice in the pictures. Ask: What are the people doing in the pictures? Where do they live? Have you ever done anything like what they are doing? Is this something you think all people do? Why? Does this remind you of anything you have ever seen before? How?	I started with this activity to engage students in drawing conclusions about people from around the world. I purposefully chose pictures that showed people working together or interacting in some other way and tried to steer the discussion toward ideas about communities (people being and working together, helping one another).

LESSON SEQUENCE AND DESCRIPTION	TEACHER COMMENTARY
Community pictures pre-assessment activity in small, mixed-readiness groups. Next, break the class into small groups of three to four students. Distribute one picture of a community scene to each group. Using a round robin format, each student in the group will write a descriptive sentence about what is happening in the group's picture.	I used mixed-readiness groups so that my students could learn from one another and help each other with the writing aspect of this activity.
While students work, move among the groups, taking notes on what students are saying,	This was an informal pre-assessment of the students' understandings about communities.
Concluding discussion. Have the groups share their picture and sentences with the class. Then ask the students to discuss similarities that the all groups observed in the scenes. What big statements can they make about communities based on their pictures?	Again, the goal here was to have the students learn from each other. Throughout the discussion, I drew on the cultural differences in my class-room by asking leading questions like, "How is your family or neighbor-hood similar to what is going on in this picture?"
Post the unit generalizations so that all can see them. Ask students if they agree or disagree with the statements. Why? How do the pictures support their arguments?	I took notes about my students' think-ing and kept the unit generalizations posted throughout the unit so that we could refer back to them often.

LESSON 2   **Who? What? Where?**   *(1 class period)*

LESSON SEQUENCE AND DESCRIPTION	TEACHER COMMENTARY
Note: Prior to this lesson, write each of the following ques-tions on two index cards (you should have total of six cards): • Who lives in a community? • What things do you see in a community? • Where can you go in a community?	
Thinking map activity in mixed-readiness (random) groups. Divide the class into six groups. Give each group one 11" x 18" piece of light-colored construction paper and one of the "question" index cards.	I designed this activity to highlight the range of people and places a com-munity contains.
Tell the groups to glue the index card onto the middle of their construction paper. The groups will answer their questions by creating thinking maps using only magazines and newspapers.	Incidentally, thinking maps are great activities for visual learners!

LESSON SEQUENCE AND DESCRIPTION	TEACHER COMMENTARY
As the groups work, circulate among them so that you can listen to the students' ideas, monitor their behavior, and do some informal assessment of their knowledge of basic terms and understandings about communities.	I reinforced students and groups who were working well and asked some probing questions: "Why are you cutting that out? Do you think that might fit better with another group? Why?"
Concluding discussion. When all groups have completed their work, hang the thinking maps in the classroom and lead a whole-group discussion about them. Ask: What do we know about communities now? What do you think are the most important parts of communities? Why do you say so?	Once again, the discussion format gave my students a chance to listen to and learn from each other.

LESSON 3 — Needs, Wants, and Unequal Resources *(3–4 class periods)*

LESSON SEQUENCE AND DESCRIPTION	TEACHER COMMENTARY
Needs simulation activity in mixed-readiness (random) groups. Divide the class into four groups. Each will receive an envelope with their group number on it containing specific materials. All of the groups will lack materials that they will need, and some will have more of a particular material than they need. Here is the distribution list: • Group 1: Two pairs of scissors, 20 paper clips, 2 pencils, and 1 piece of white construction paper. • Group 2: One glue stick, two sheets of green construction paper, two sheets of brown construction paper, and two sheets of blue construction paper • Group 3: Three pieces of white construction paper, one sheet of green construction paper, one sheet of brown construction paper. • Group 4: One pair of scissors, one piece of blue construction paper, one ruler.	I adapted this activity from the California Council for Social Studies *Sunburst,* February 1984, as I knew my students would enjoy its hands-on focus. It also reinforced the idea that people in a community often have to work together to meet their needs.
All groups will complete the same series of tasks. Display the tasks on an overhead and/or distribute a copy to each group: • *Food:* Make four strips of green paper, each four inches long. • *Clothing:* Make a blue "T-shirt." • *Shelter:* Make a white square and attach a brown triangle to one side. • *Education:* Make a four-page book using two different colors. • *Interdependence:* Make a four-link paper chain using four different colors.	The frustration the students felt when they realized they didn't have all the materials they needed to complete the tasks led them to find ways to solve their "problems"—illustrating our unit concept of **interdependence.**

LESSON SEQUENCE AND DESCRIPTION	TEACHER COMMENTARY
Observe the students as they interact, and note ways in which they demonstrate cooperation and **interdependence**.	I circulated around the room to keep students on task and provide feedback. When groups seemed stuck, I asked cueing questions: "What do you do when you don't have something you need?" "What's the best way to get something you need?"
Once the students have completed their tasks, distribute the following discussion questions and give the groups time to talk about them. 1. Could you have completed your tasks without getting materials from another group? 2. How did your group adapt to not having all of the materials you needed? 3. Were there conflicts between groups? Why? 4. Which group finished first? Why? 5. Were there differences in the ways the groups finished their tasks? Why?	
Discussion of needs simulation activity. Allow the small groups to share some of their responses to the discussion questions. How does this activity relate to communities? What can we conclude about communities? Encourage students to use the terms *needs* and *resources* as they discuss their group work and observations.	This was a good place to take a look back at the unit generalizations: "Which big ideas have we worked with today? How do you know?"
Tiered writing prompts based on readiness. Assign students to one of the following writing prompts. Students will answer their prompts independently. *Prompt 1 (Lower Readiness)* What are some needs that you have in the classroom? For instance, what do you need to get your work done? Do you always have everything that you need? How are your needs met in the classroom?	Tiering these prompts enabled me to address different readiness levels. I assigned prompts based on the students' ability to apply the lesson's ideas beyond our classroom. Note that I didn't automatically assign ESL or LD students to Prompt 1. I assigned this prompt to concrete thinkers not yet ready to apply ideas more broadly. The classroom is a very familiar place—one that students are usually very comfortable talking about.

LESSON SEQUENCE AND DESCRIPTION	TEACHER COMMENTARY
Prompt 2 (Higher Readiness) What are some needs that your family has? Where does your family go to make sure those needs are met? Who helps your family meet its needs?	This second, more challenging prompt was designed for students who need more abstract application. It asks students to transfer their understanding beyond our immediate environment. Here, they were not just thinking about themselves, but about their families.
Sharing of written responses and discussion of needs versus wants. Allow the students to share their writing with partners.	This gave the students a chance to add to their own ideas by listening to others.
Then ask the whole group to reflect upon what they identified as needs. Are some of their *needs* really *wants?* What's the difference between the two? Can something be both a need and a want? Create a class list of needs and wants and post it in the classroom.	The difference between needs and wants can be a difficult concept for elementary-age children. I wanted to address it directly.
Independent or partner work on tasks based on Sternberg's triarchic intelligences. Students will select one of the following tasks to complete either independently or with a partner:	I used Sternberg's theory here because I like to vary my approach as much as possible and because it provides different ways for students to examine needs and wants and their roles in our lives.
Task 1: Practical Intelligence Create an advice column for people who don't understand the difference between needs and wants. Write their letters to you (at least three) as well as your answers back to them. The people writing to you really need your help because they are confusing their needs and their wants. Make sure that your advice to them is clear and useful.	
Task 2: Analytical Intelligence Make your own personal lists of needs and wants. What are your needs and wants? How do you know the difference? Include at least five things on each list. Then order the items on your lists from most important to least important. What is your most important need? Most important want? Write an argument that explains why you ranked your needs and wants the way you did.	

LESSON SEQUENCE AND DESCRIPTION	TEACHER COMMENTARY
Task 3: Creative Intelligence Create a story about a person's needs and wants. Who is this person? What needs and wants does he or she have and how are they met? What happens when they are not met? Make your story original and funny. How you present your story is up to you.	
Product sharing and closure activity. Provide time for the students to share their products with their classmates. Then, give each student an index card and tell the students to write their names, two of their needs, and two of their wants on their cards.	This quick way of assessing whether or not the students understood the difference between needs and wants also allowed them to relate to these concepts personally. After this activity, I met with some students individually or in small groups to provide further coaching on this concept.

LESSON 4   *Roxaboxen*   *(1–2 class periods)*

LESSON SEQUENCE AND DESCRIPTION	TEACHER COMMENTARY
Review of needs and wants and introduction of community resources. Begin the lesson by telling the students that today they will discover more about communities. Review the terms *need* and *want*. Share some of the students' responses from the index cards (Lesson 3) concerning their needs and wants. Ask: How might you get what you need or want? Where would you go in the community to meet this need or want? Who in the community might be able to meet your need? Your want? Point out that communities have **resources** that are used to meet people's needs and wants—for example, their need for health care. Ask: What resources in our community provide health care? (Hospitals, doctors and nurses, etc.) What other community resources can you think of that meet our particular wants and needs? Make sure that the students understand that both places and people can be community **resources**.	As often as possible, I like to use the students' ideas as "teachable moments." Here, I began to connect the previous lesson on needs and wants with the idea of community resources, using our community as the prime example.
Reading and discussion of *Roxaboxen*. Read Alice McLerran's *Roxaboxen* aloud for the group, and then discuss the book with the class.	This book is a great one for exploring the idea of community.

LESSON SEQUENCE AND DESCRIPTION	TEACHER COMMENTARY
Ask: Is Roxaboxen a community? Why? What community resources did the children create in Roxaboxen? What do you like about Roxaboxen? What would you change about it?	I asked my students questions that were open-ended enough to invite a range of possible responses. I wanted them to respond to the story on a personal level before they began their independent or small-group work.
Tiered activities based on readiness. All students will work with the idea that needs in a community are met by particular resources. Assign students to one of the following tasks:	I knew my students had different readiness levels (based on formal measures such as tests and informal ones such as discussions) with regard to understanding and responding to literature, and that to engage and challenge them all, I needed to allow them to approach this lesson's concept in different ways. Thus, tiered assignments were in order.
Task 1 (Struggling Learners) You will work as a group with the teacher to reread and discuss the story. Then you will complete a chart showing community resources in Roxaboxen and the needs those resources meet.	This first task is concrete and structured. I led the discussion and then provided guidance and prompt questions as needed.
Task 2 (On-Target Learners) The children in the story worked hard to create different community resources in Roxaboxen, but did they find a way to meet all the needs of all the people? Make a list of at least five needs that are not met in Roxaboxen, and then explain how those needs might be met in the community. What else do the children need to create? You may work alone or with a partner to complete this assignment.	The second task is appropriate for learners who can grasp the story and work without direct assistance. Although it's more open-ended than the first task, the product format (a list) provides a degree of structure.
Task 3 (Advanced Learners) The community in *Roxaboxen* was created by children. What if it had been created by adults? Would it have the same community resources and community places? Find a way to show your classmates what Roxaboxen might have looked like if it had been created by adults instead of children. What different things would you find in the community? You will work in pairs to complete this task. Be ready to explain your work and your thinking.	The third task is the most abstract and open-ended of the three assignments, requiring students to compare the perspectives of children and adults to determine differences in their needs. Note that the product format is unspecified. I asked students to work in pairs so that they could discuss and evaluate their thinking as they prepared their products (a good way to build metacognitive skills!).

LESSON SEQUENCE AND DESCRIPTION	TEACHER COMMENTARY
Product sharing and related discussion in small, mixed-readiness groups. Students will meet in small groups to share their work with one another and to discuss different community resources. Do they know people who are community resources in their own community? What about some places that are resources?	Sharing products in mixed-readiness groups provides validation and reinforces the idea that everyone has something important to contribute. Here, I gave the groups specific instructions on how to share their work. I also moved among the groups and posed questions to extend their thinking.

LESSON 5   Interviewing a Community Helper   *(5–6 class periods)*

LESSON SEQUENCE AND DESCRIPTION	TEACHER COMMENTARY
Think–Pair–Share: Community helpers. As a class and using Think–Pair–Share, create a list of the roles that are filled in a community (for example, grocer, florist, letter carrier). Have students first think on their own, then discuss their ideas with another student sitting next to them, and finally, share their ideas with the whole group. Write their ideas on a list and post the list of community helpers for all to see.	I find that the Think–Pair–Share format encourages a greater number of student responses than simply using a whole-group discussion format. It is also more likely to encourage students of a broad range of readiness levels to participate actively. This would also be a good time to discuss whether roles are similar or dissimilar in other cultures with which students might be familiar.
Interview tasks based on readiness and learning profile. When the students have added all of their ideas to the list, tell them that they will be interviewing a community helper about his or her role in the community. All students must come up with interview questions and must research a community helper of their choosing. Be sure to provide books and Web sites at a variety of reading levels that will help the students with their research. Explain to students that they will be imagining what the community helper might say in response to a set of interview questions.	I assigned students to particular interview tasks based on readiness. Then I asked students to choose a product option, allowing them to work in a preferred modality. As needed, I provided miniworkshops on interviewing skills and gave the students the chance to conduct practice interviews with one another.

LESSON SEQUENCE AND DESCRIPTION	TEACHER COMMENTARY
Students will work in assigned pairs based on their interest in particular community helpers to create their imaginary interviews. In their pairs, they will collaborate to discuss possible questions and to research how their community helpers would respond to those questions.	Working with an English-speaking partner is a good option for students who might struggle with this activity due to limited language skills and experience.
When it comes time to prepare the interview questions, divide students into two groups: • Group 1 will participate in a teacher-led brainstorming session to create a list of good interview questions. Each student in the group will select questions from this list. • Group 2 will work independently, with each student creating his or her own interview questions.	Some students didn't know where to begin with this task, while others had a very clear idea of what they wanted to find out. I worked with the first group of students to help them generate interview questions and allowed the second group to create questions on their own.
Group 1 (Lower Readiness) From the list of interview questions we brainstormed, choose 5 to 10 questions that you will pose to the community helper you will be interviewing. Be ready to explain how you decided which questions to use. How will your community helper respond?	Some of the sample questions I provided included, "How did school prepare you for your job?" and "Who helps you in your job?"
Group 2 (Higher Readiness) Create a list of questions that you will ask your community helper. What kinds of questions will tell you the most about this person and his or her role in the community? How will he or she respond to these questions? Your job is to make us see why this person is important to a community.	I allowed some of the Group 2 students to work together to finalize their questions. Although I'd like for all of my students to be able to work as independently as possible, I recognize that some students need more support than others.
Products from interviews based on Gardner's multiple intelligences. Students in both groups will then create an individual product demonstrating how the role of his or her chosen community helper interacts with or affects other community roles. They will choose from the following product options: *Product Option 1: Visual/Spatial and Verbal/Linguistic Intelligence* Create a poster that shows the community helper and how he or she responded during the "interview." *Product Option 2: Verbal/Linguistic and Visual/Spatial Intelligence* Make an audiotape or videotape of your "interview."	I designed these options to allow students to choose products suited to their different learning profiles. Due to the nature of the interview assignment, all the product options also draw on interpersonal intelligence.

LESSON SEQUENCE AND DESCRIPTION	TEACHER COMMENTARY
Product Option 3: Musical Intelligence Write and perform a song about the community helper, based on your "interview." *Product Option 4: Visual/Spatial Intelligence* Create a collage about the community helper based on the "interview."	
Product sharing and discussion. Students will share their products with the class. As they do so, invite the students to further examine the specific role that a community helper plays in their community. How does _____ provide for or help our community? What might happen if he or she was no longer here or could not do his or her job?	This was another chance for the students to learn from one another. Although I could have given my students all the information about different community helpers, the process of conducting research and an interview allowed each student to become an "expert" about a specific community helper. Plus, it's a much more engaging approach.
Tiered writing prompts based on writing and thinking skills readiness. Assign students one of the following persuasive writing prompts:	These readiness-based prompts provide all students with a chance to evaluate the roles that community helpers play, but acknowledge that students' writing abilities can vary greatly. I coached students for quality responses whatever their level of writing proficiency.
Prompt 1 (Lower Readiness) Who do you think is the most important community helper? Using the list we made in class, select one community helper and come up with three reasons why he or she is the most important person in the community. Write three sentences that explain your thinking and that will persuade others to agree with you.	The first prompt was designed for students who find writing sentences a challenge.
Prompt 2 (Higher Readiness) Who do you think is the most important community helper? Give five reasons in a well-written and organized paragraph for why you think the way that you do. Be specific! And remember: You are trying to get us to agree with you!	The second prompt is appropriate for students who are able to put sentences together to create paragraphs.

LESSON SEQUENCE AND DESCRIPTION	TEACHER COMMENTARY
Prompt 3 (Highest Readiness) Some contributions to communities might be seen as more important than others while other contributions might be more creative. Choose a community helper whose role is the most important and one whose role you think is the most creative. Write a paper of more than one paragraph that convinces others to agree with you.	The third prompt is more open-ended and abstract than the first two, and it requires strong writing skills. Sometimes I find I need to talk with the students responding to this prompt about what creativity is: "When is something creative? When are you being creative?"
Sharing and discussion of written responses. Allow the students to share their ideas with one another. How many students think the _____ is the most important community helper? Why? Is one community helper really more important than all of the others? Are there any that are less important? What might happen if a particular community helper had to leave the community and his or her role was left empty? For example, what if your community did not have a vet? A plumber?	My goal for this discussion was to help students pull together all that that they had learned about community helpers and to invite evaluative thinking.
Close the discussion by referring back to the unit generalizations about **interdependence**. Ask: Which ones have we worked with during this lesson? How do you know?	I wanted to ensure that the students incorporated the unit's important ideas.

LESSON 6　　　　　　**A Kinesthetic Simulation**　　　　*(1 class period)*

LESSON SEQUENCE AND DESCRIPTION	TEACHER COMMENTARY
Note: For this lesson, write the names of community helpers from Lesson 5's class-generated list on slips of paper. Add additional helpers if necessary until there are the same number of "helper slips" as there are students in the class.	
Interdependence simulation activity. Introduce this lesson by asking the students if they have any questions about the previous lesson. Then put the slips of paper with community helper names in a hat or bag and ask each student to draw one name.	I knew that after the rigors of the previous lesson, my students would appreciate a shorter activity that provides engagement through movement and interaction. This is particularly important for students who really struggle with writing, for those who don't sit still easily, and for those who learn best kinesthetically. This is a great activity to do outside.

LESSON SEQUENCE AND DESCRIPTION	TEACHER COMMENTARY
Next, have the students stand in a circle and put their hands on the shoulders of the person in front of them. Tell them to sit on the lap of the person behind them when you say "Go." Stress that all of the students must sit at the *same time*. Once the students have mastered sitting without falling, explain that as members of a community, each of them has a particular role to play. Go around the circle and have students say the name of the role they're playing. Then explain that you are going to tell them different stories and that each of them must listen closely for their cue to "leave the community." Provide scenarios that result in community helpers having to leave the community or stop working. For example: "Our town's children's doctor has gotten sick and must take several weeks off from work. Children's doctor, please leave the community." When the student representing this role leaves the circle, the rest of the group will find it's much more difficult to accomplish the goal of sitting. Repeat this procedure several times and then discuss what has been happening. Is there one role in a community that could be removed without impacting the community? Why or why not?	
Pair work on cause and effect based on student choice. Students will work in pairs to create/fill in a **Community Helper Cause-and-Effect Graphic Organizer** (see Sample 3.2, page 93) that shows what happens when a particular community helper (of their choosing) can no longer play his or her role in the community.	For this task, I allowed students to choose the person they wanted to work with because they had not been able to do so in a while. I provided a sample map-style graphic organizer to encourage the students to think broadly.
Discussion of unit generalizations. Wrap up the lesson by looking once again at the unit generalizations. Ask: Which generalizations do you agree with now? Why? How does our group activity relate to the big ideas we've been discussing?	Again, I brought the unit's big ideas to students' attention and gave them the chance to draw new conclusions based on classroom activities.

LESSON 7	**Concluding Activity**	*(1 class period)*

LESSON SEQUENCE AND DESCRIPTION	TEACHER COMMENTARY
Independent completion of RAFT activities based on learning profile and Gardner's multiple intelligences. As part of the assessment for this unit, students choose and complete one of the **Community RAFT Activity Options** (see Sample 3.3, page 94). Explain to the students that they will work on their products independently. Before students begin work, explain that their work will be evaluated based on the following criteria: • Accuracy regarding information about specific community helpers • Thoughtfulness • Originality (Use your own ideas!) • Neatness (Make a draft first!) • Time in class spent wisely	The RAFT activity options address different learning profiles (the list and set of directions focus on logical/ mathematical thinking while the letter and the speech require verbal/linguistic skill) but do so at similar readiness levels. I asked the students to choose the activity that would show their best work and thinking. I find that better work results when I share the evaluation criteria with my students *before* they begin.

LESSON 8	**Unit Assessment**	*(1 class period)*

LESSON SEQUENCE AND DESCRIPTION	TEACHER COMMENTARY
Independent completion of unit final assessment questions. Students will compete an assessment of what they have come to understand throughout this unit. Questions on the assessment include the following: • How is our school a community? • What needs are present in our school community? • Who are some community helpers in our school community? What do they do? • Choose two people in our school community. Explain their roles in our school community and tell what would happen to our school if they were no longer a part of the community. • How does our school community show **interdependence**?	This assessment is more structured than the RAFT options in Lesson 7. I wanted my students to try to transfer what they had learned during this unit to a situation we hadn't discussed at great length. By focusing on the school community, the students could work with something they knew well. I allowed students to write *and* draw in response to the questions, and I presented some students with only one question at a time so that they wouldn't be overwhelmed by seeing them all at once.

Teacher Reflection on the Unit

Looking at communities through the concept of interdependence is interesting and challenging for me as a teacher. So is finding meaningful and responsive ways to connect students' lives to the state curriculum. The first time my students began to make connections between the ideas they were learning in these lessons and their lives outside of our classroom and school, I knew the unit was a success. Each time I present this unit, my students particularly enjoy the Community Learning Contract (they love making choices!) as well as the many opportunities for group work. I've found that focusing on my students' interests and learning preferences leads to increased engagement for them and greater insight for me: I'm able to learn a lot about them based on the choices that they make.

Jennifer Ann Bonnett has degrees in general and special education and has taught elementary students in Rhode Island and North Carolina. She can be reached at jenniferbonn@yahoo.com.

SAMPLE 3.1—Differentiated Community Learning Contracts

Community Learning Contract (RED)

Read through the list of activities and choose three (or more!) to complete on your own. When you have decided on the activities you would like to complete, please fill out, sign, and turn in the Learning Contract Agreement at the end of this document.

You may work on your activities when you have finished work and when I give you time to do so in class. You may also have to do some work outside of class, but I'd like for you to do most of your work in class. I'll ask you to share your work with your classmates, so be ready to do so!

❑ **Name That Place!**
Brainstorm 10 types of businesses that you would find in a community (for example, a grocery store, a flower shop, a veterinarian's office). Then use the Yellow Pages to find a specific business in our community that fits each type. Make a list of the businesses and their phone numbers. Choose one of the businesses and draw a picture of what you think might go on there during a typical day. Who works there? What tools or objects do they use to do their jobs?

❑ **Community Scavenger Hunt**
Using all available resources, find 10 items on the following list. If the item asks you to find information (such as the names and addresses of businesses or people or a certain kind of business), write it in next to that item. When the item asks you to find a person, please ask him or her to sign your list next to the appropriate item.

- Person who sells a product. _____
- Person who provides a service. _____
- Person who has lived in our community for more than 20 years. _____
- Street where you'd find the town hall. _____
- Name and address of a museum. _____
- Name and address of a bank. _____
- A famous local landmark. Write in the name and, below, what makes it famous. (_____)
- Best pizza in town. _____
- Best ice cream in town. _____
- Name of a local park. _____
- A busy street corner. _____

- An Italian restaurant.   _____
- A Mexican restaurant.   _____
- A building that has been in the community for more than 50 years.   _____
- Name of the mayor.   _____
- Name of the police chief.   _____

If you want to find more items, go for it! List everything you find and get signatures when appropriate.

❏   **Community Survey/Poster**

Survey your classmates to find out the following:

- Favorite restaurant.
- Favorite park.
- Favorite store.

First, decide how you will find out the information. Will you ask your classmates or will you create a written survey to give to them? How will you keep track of their responses? Finally, make a poster that shows your classmates' favorite places in the community.

❏   **Community ABCs**

Make an ABC list about our community. Make sure that you have a place, business, or person's name for each letter of the alphabet.

❏   **Under Construction**

Using the Community software,* follow the directions to design a building for a community. Once you have completed your building, print it out and write about why it is an important building for a community. What is the name of the building? What makes it unique? How does it meet the needs of people living in a community?

❏   **Community Collage**

Using photographs and pictures from magazines, newspapers, and the Internet, create a collage of at least 10 things that you think make our community special. Then, write a "museum sign" to go next to your collage explaining what you have chosen to include in it and why.

_____

*Stearns, P. H., & Nolan, S. (1998). Community Construction Kit [Computer Software]. Watertown, MA: Tom Snyder Productions.

SAMPLE 3.1—*(continued)*

Learning Contract Agreement

I, _____ , agree to work on the following activities (must choose at least three from the list of options) during the Community unit:

1.

2.

3.

4.

I understand that my work will be evaluated based on the following criteria:

- Neatness
- Thoughtfulness
- Accuracy of information
- Originality (if appropriate)

I understand my contract work must be turned in by the following date: _____ .

I will work on the contract activities that I select during class time unless I first discuss with my teacher doing something outside of class.

I agree to stay on task while working on my contract activities so that I do not distract others and so that I can put forth my best effort.

Student's Signature _____ Date _____

Teacher's Signature _____ Date _____

SAMPLE 3.1—*(continued)*

Community Learning Contract (BLUE)

Read through the list of activities and choose three (or more!) to complete on your own. When you have decided on the activities you would like to complete, please fill out, sign, and turn in the Learning Contract Agreement at the end of this document.

You may work on your activities when you have finished work and when I give you time to do so in class. You may have to also do some work outside of class, but I'd like for you to do most of your work in class. I'll ask you to share your work with our classmates, so be ready to do so!

❏ **Name That Place!**

Brainstorm 10 types of businesses that you would find in a community (for example, a grocery store, a flower shop, a veterinarian's office). Then use the Yellow Pages to find a specific business in our community that fits each type. Make a list of the businesses and their phone numbers. Next, think of a new business that our community needs. Create a print advertisement (like one you might find in a newspaper) for this new business. What is its name? Why should people in the community use this business? What makes it better than other similar businesses? What makes it special or unique?

❏ **Community Scavenger Hunt**

Using all available resources, find examples of the items on the following list. Use the space provided to explain items you identify. If you find a person to fit a particular item, please ask him or her to sign your list next to the appropriate item.

- Person who sells a product. _____
- Person who provides a service. _____
- Person who has made a difference in our community.
  How did this person make a difference? _____
- A sign of change in our community. What is changing? _____
- A problem our community has. Why is this a problem? _____
- Something that makes our community different from other
  nearby communities. _____
- A person who left and then came back to our community.
  Why did he or she return? _____
- A person who has seen the community change.
  What has this person seen? _____
- A business that has been in the community for more than 20 years.
  Why has it been able to stay open for this long? _____

SAMPLE 3.1—*(continued)*

❏ **Community Survey/Poster**

Survey at least 10 people in the community to find out the following:

- Favorite restaurant.
- Favorite building.
- Favorite veterinarian.

First, decide how you will find out the information. Will you ask you people yourself or will you create a written survey to give to them? How will you keep track of their responses? Finally, make a poster that shows favorite places in the community.

❏ **Under Construction**

Using the Community software, follow the directions to design a building for a community. Once you have completed your building, print it out and write about why it is an important building for a community. What is the name of the building? What makes it unique? How does it meet the needs of people living in a community? What roles will people who work in the building play in the community?

❏ **Come Visit Our Community!**

Using information from resources provided in the classroom and that you can find elsewhere, as well as examples of various travel brochures (which I will provide), create a travel brochure about our community. Your brochure should make people outside of our community want to come visit it. How will you make our community seem special? What are some of the best things you can say about our community? Be sure to use pictures and words to make your brochure attractive and professional looking.

SAMPLE 3.1—*(continued)*

Learning Contract Agreement

I, _____ , agree to work on the following activities (must choose at least three from the list of options) during the Community unit:

1.

2.

3.

4.

I understand that my work will be evaluated based on the following criteria:

• Neatness
• Thoughtfulness
• Accuracy of information
• Originality (if appropriate)

I understand my contract work must be turned in by the following date: _____ .

I will work on the contract activities that I select during class time unless I first discuss with my teacher doing something outside of class.

I agree to stay on task while working on my contract activities so that I do not distract others and so that I can put forth my best effort.

Student's Signature _____ Date _____

Teacher's Signature _____ Date _____

SAMPLE 3.2—Community Helper Cause-and-Effect Graphic Organizer

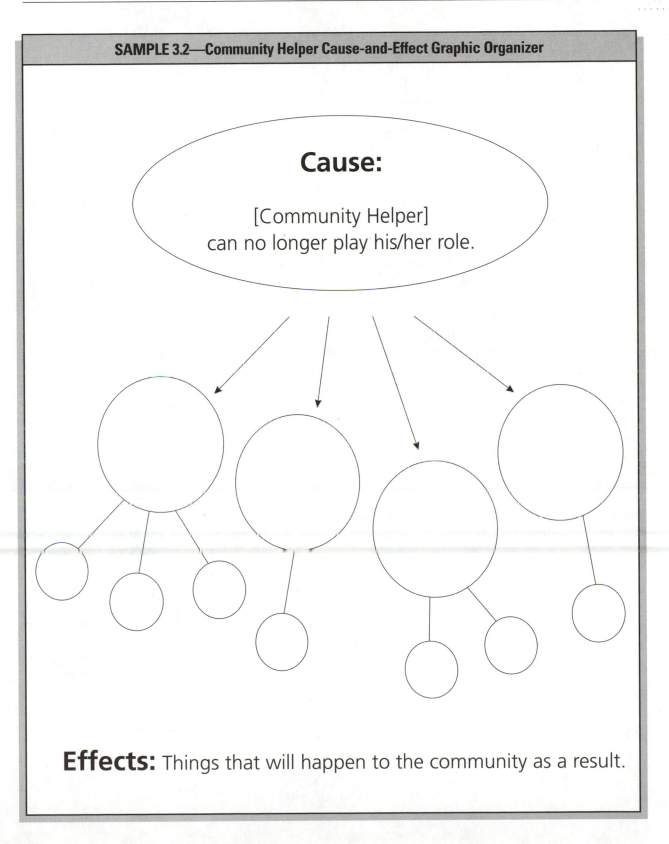

Cause:

[Community Helper]
can no longer play his/her role.

Effects: Things that will happen to the community as a result.

SAMPLE 3.3—Community RAFT Activity Options

Role	Audience	Format	Topic
2nd grader	1st graders	Top 10 list in order of importance	Community Helpers
One community helper	Another community helper	Letter	Why I Am More Important Than You
Community helper	Community	Speech	Why You Can't Do Without Me
2nd grader	Newcomer to the community	How-to list or set of directions	How to Get Your Needs Met in Our Community

4

The World of Geometry

*A Mathematics Unit on
Basic Geometric Concepts*

Unit Developer: Elizabeth Hargrave

Introduction

This three- to four-week geometry unit, based on state standards and competency goals for elementary mathematics, focuses on a "hands-on" look at lines, angles, shapes, and their attributes as they apply to the students' environment. The goal is to give students an understanding of basic geometric concepts, especially as they apply to real-life situations.

The unit begins with a pre-assessment to gauge students' starting readiness levels and culminates with the creation of final products that require students to apply what they have learned. Throughout, students are encouraged to think of geometry as an integral part of the world around them and to see geometric terms as having a communicative value that extends beyond the classroom. Although the unit is intended to extend over three or four weeks, its actual length may vary depending upon how much class time is spent working on the final products.

Teacher Reflection on Designing the Unit

As I began planning this unit, I thought about the wide variety of background knowledge students bring to math class. In the context of geometry, I knew some of my students would have little recollection of any previous exposure to geometric terms and concepts beyond simple shape recognition. Other students would already have demonstrated solid mastery of the geometry goals beyond their current grade level. Of course, the majority of students would be somewhere on a continuum between these two extremes.

Because of this range of familiarity with geometry, I knew I needed to be thinking in terms of differentiating many of the unit's lessons and activities. Interest and learning-style surveys given at the beginning of the year, along with observation and consistent anecdotal records, had supplied me with information about individual students' preferred approaches to learning tasks, as well as their areas of special interest. I wanted to take these learning styles and interest areas into consideration when selecting and planning activities for this geometry unit.

It has been my experience that with increased emphasis on end-of-grade testing and state pacing guides, elementary-level geometry units usually receive cursory attention, with students given less time than I think they need to manipulate and examine the ideas and concepts presented. With this unit, I wanted to make sure my students had lots of opportunities to handle and explore objects in their environment as we studied geometric terms and the attributes of those objects. I also wanted to stay away from the "worksheet approach" to geometry as much as possible. I believe that if students are actively involved and engaged in learning tasks, especially ones that involve manipulatives, their learning will transfer to more traditional paper-and-pencil activities or test questions when needed. With this in mind, as I planned this unit I gathered a variety of manipulatives (including measurement tools, Geoboards, cardboard, and net figures) that students could use to further their understanding and skills.

Geometry has been a passion of mine from youth. I agree with educator Dr. George Macfeely Conwell who said, "The study of geometry is especially fitted to the youthful mind. It encourages the development of intelligence, imagination and diligence." My hope in creating this unit was to convey my enthusiasm for the subject and to have my students come away with the understanding that the study of geometry can be relevant and useful to their lives.

Mathematics Standards Addressed

Measurement and Geometry. The learner will recognize, understand, and use basic geometric properties and standard units of metric and customary measurement:

- Draw and classify polygons and polyhedrons (solid figures) using appropriate vocabulary: *faces, angles, edges,* and *vertices.* Describe rules for grouping.
- Identify and model symmetry and congruence with concrete materials and drawing.
- Recognize three-dimensional objects from different perspectives.
- Observe and describe geometry in the environment.

Unit Concepts and Generalizations
Structure

- There is structure in everything around us.
- Structure helps us define and categorize objects in our world.
- Structure is often based on patterns of parts that create a whole.
- The structure of some objects can be explained in geometrical terms.

Unit Objectives

As a result of this unit, the students will *know*

- The attributes of points, lines, line segments, planes, rays, parallel lines, and perpendicular lines.
- Types of angles (right angle, acute angle, obtuse angle).
- The unique characteristics of circles and their related parts (radius, diameter, circumference, chord).
- What makes shapes and objects congruent and symmetrical.
- The distinguishing characteristics of the following polyhedrons: cone, cube, pyramid, rectangular prism, cylinder, and triangular prism.
- Different rules for grouping polygons and polyhedrons using the following terms: *faces, angles, edges,* and *vertices.*

As a result of this unit, the students will *understand that*

- The shortest distance between two points is a straight line.
- Geometry and symmetry are found in nature.
- There is a structure to everything around us.
- Using geometric terms is one way to describe the structure of our environment.
- Geometry is a very important part of the building industry and of architecture, art, science, astronomy, clothing design, farming, and many other professions.
- There is often a relationship between the shape of an object and its use.

As a result of this unit, the students will *be able to*

- Describe, draw, compare, and classify geometric objects.
- Communicate effectively using geometric terms.
- Gather, analyze, and apply geometric information in problem solving.
- Work cooperatively in pairs and small groups.
- Establish a project plan, including a timeline, and follow it.

Instructional Strategies Used

- Brainstorming
- Flexible grouping
- Independent projects with process logs and a scoring rubric
- RAFT activities
- Think–Pair–Share
- Differentiated writing prompts
- Gardner's multiple intelligences
- Pre-assessment
- Small-group collaborative activities
- Tiered assignments

Sample Supporting Materials Provided

Unit Overview

LESSON	WHOLE-CLASS COMPONENTS	DIFFERENTIATED COMPONENTS
LESSON 1 **Introduction** *1 class period*	Discussion in List–Group–Label format *20 minutes* Writing activity as pre-assessment *15–20 minutes*	
LESSON 2 **Points, Lines, Line Segments, and Rays** *1 class period*	Discussion of definitions and examples *10–15 minutes* Small-group problem solving *30 minutes* Whole-group sharing for lesson closure. *10 minutes*	
LESSON 3 **Angles** *2–3 class periods*	Discussion of the types of angles and demonstration of angle measurement *15 minutes* Practice identifying and measuring angles in small, mixed-readiness groups *20 minutes* Discussion for lesson closure *5–10 minutes*	Tiered assignment based on readiness *50–75 minutes*

LESSON	WHOLE-CLASS COMPONENTS	DIFFERENTIATED COMPONENTS
LESSON 4 **Circles** *1–2 class periods*	Reading assignment on circles and discussion *15–20 minutes* Partner discussions of circles *10 minutes* Discussion for lesson closure *5–10 minutes*	 Journal prompts differentiated by readiness *30 minutes*
LESSON 5 **Polygons** *1 class period*	Discussion of the prefixes, names, and attributes of polygons *15 minutes* Geoboard activity *40 minutes* Discussion for lesson closure *5–10 minutes*	
LESSON 6 **Tangrams** *2–3 class periods*	Presentation of basic tangram shapes *5 minutes* Reading and discussion of *Grandfather Tang's Story* *20–30 minutes* Product sharing and discussion for lesson closure *10–15 minutes*	 Tiered tangram activities based on readiness *60 minutes*
LESSON 7 **Symmetry and Congruence** *1–2 class periods*	Discussion of and practice with finding lines of symmetry in classroom objects and in the alphabet *30 minutes* Small-group practice with polygon symmetry *20 minutes*	

LESSON	WHOLE-CLASS COMPONENTS	DIFFERENTIATED COMPONENTS
	Introduction of congruent shapes using Geoboards *30 minutes*	
	Exit card activity for lesson closure *5 minutes*	
LESSON 8 **Observing and Describing Geometry in Flags** *1–2 class periods*	Round robin review in mixed-readiness groups *20 minutes*	
	Discussion of shapes in state and country flags *15 minutes*	
		Tiered task card activities based on readiness *40–45 minutes*
	Small- and large-group discussions for lesson closure *10–15 minutes*	
LESSON 9 **Polyhedrons** *1–2 class periods*	Discussion of the attributes of polyhedrons *15 minutes*	
	Think–Pair–Share: Is a sphere a polyhedron? *10 minutes*	
	Small-group activity with the vocabulary of polyhedrons *15 minutes*	
		Self-selected application tasks based on Gardner's multiple intelligences *40 minutes*
	Product sharing with partners *10 minutes*	
	3–2–1 exit card activity for lesson closure *5 minutes*	

LESSON	WHOLE-CLASS COMPONENTS	DIFFERENTIATED COMPONENTS
LESSON 10 **Review and Application** *2–3 class periods*	Polyhedron review *10 minutes*	
	Geometry scavenger hunt in mixed-readiness groups *40 minutes*	
		Self-selected RAFT activities based on interest and learning style *45–60 minutes*
LESSON 11 **Unit Assessment** *1–2 class periods*		Self-selected final products based on student interest and learning style *1–2 class periods*

Unit Pre-Assessment: Geometry Knowledge Rating Scale

Prior to beginning this unit, take a quick baseline assessment of what your students think they already know about the subject of geometry. Lead a brief discussion of geometry vocabulary to jog the students' memories. Then make a **Geometry Knowledge Rating Scale** (see Sample 4.1, page 120) on poster board or chart paper and place it on the classroom wall in an accessible spot. Under the chart, leave a stack of color-coded labels (sticky-backed colored circles). Ask the students to take one sticker and place it above the category title that best describes their level of geometry knowledge. (This is best done at snack or break time so that everyone is not at the chart at the same time.) Remind students to try to honestly assess what they feel they know about the subject. The result will be a colorful bar graph of the students' range of prior knowledge levels.

Teacher Reflection on the Unit Pre-Assessment

My primary goal with all assessment data (whether formal, informal, or a combination of both) is to use it to make appropriate decisions about instruction so that all of my students, no matter what their readiness levels, have an opportunity to grow during the course of a unit. At the beginning of new units, I frequently use a Knowledge Rating Scale to assess prior knowledge levels of the class as a whole. This scale is an adaptation of the business tool called a *consensogram*. It is simply a chart with different levels of knowledge listed. As described, students rate their level of knowledge about the subject by placing a colored sticky circle above one of the categories. Neither the teacher nor the students are to make any comment regarding circle placements. The circles do not have names on them, so there is no way for students to know who placed the circles in the various categories.

I find that once instructed about how to place their circle, students give more candid assessments if the activity is done during a break time or some time during the day when there may only be one or two students at the chart at one time. For the most part, students tend to be realistic about their understanding of a subject. I have also found that the more I use this tool, the better the class becomes at assessing their own knowledge levels.

This type of chart is not only helpful in assessing prior knowledge of the class, but it also helps students understand data collecting and graphing. The chart also provides a visual reminder to students that they all will need to work on different activities from time to time throughout the unit. You can also use the scale again at the end of the unit for a quick assessment of change in class knowledge levels. This scale gives me an idea of the class's overall competency and of the range of competencies in my classroom. During a unit's first lesson, I find out more about individual students' competencies through a class brainstorming activity. If I need more information, I know that I can always give a more formal paper-and-pencil assessment.

With this geometry unit, when I find students who clearly "already get" much of what I am presenting, I allow them to start on the final products early, and I adjust my expectations for their products based on the additional time they spend working on them. For students who have severe learning problems, I work with a specialist to set reasonable goals (for example, naming shapes), and I find time to work with them individually or in small groups.

Unit Description and Teacher Commentary

LESSON 1	Introduction	*(1 class period)*
LESSON SEQUENCE AND DESCRIPTION		TEACHER COMMENTARY
Discussion in List–Group–Label format. Begin the unit with a whole-group discussion about geometry in the form of a List–Group–Label activity.		These introductory discussions served as an informal pre-assessment.
First, students will brainstorm a list of ideas about geometry. Open by asking students what they think of when they hear the word *geometry*. Record their responses on sticky notes, and place them randomly on the board or on a large piece of chart paper.		During brainstorming, it is important to accept any idea without judgment. I instructed the class to accept all ideas and listened for misunderstandings to "correct" during the course of the unit.

LESSON SEQUENCE AND DESCRIPTION	TEACHER COMMENTARY
After many ideas have been given, tell the students to categorize the terms and come up with names for their groups of terms. How can they group these terms? What will they call their groups? You may need to give a prompt for a label, such as, "Triangle, squares, and rectangles are flat figures," to get the students started.	I was looking for students' knowledge of geometric terms and concepts, and I took notes as the students offered their ideas. Did they already know types of angles, parts of a circle, names of plane and solid figures? Could they categorize shapes? I also made note of fluency of ideas and flexibility in grouping when categorizing their ideas.
Next, discuss some of the ways that geometry is used in the world. What are some jobs in which people use geometry? Again, record student responses on the board, chart paper, or an overhead.	There will always be a few students who have a good handle on the subject before you begin. (They might be the ones who responded, "Can teach the class" on the Knowledge Scale completed before the unit.) In this unit, as in others, I encouraged these students to show what they know without monopolizing the conversation or criticizing their classmates' ideas. More reluctant students often become animated and engaged during this type of brainstorming activity, especially if they feel safe to express their ideas.
Writing activity as pre-assessment. To conclude the introduction to the unit, ask the students to write one or two paragraphs about some ways they use or might use geometry in their lives. Their writing will serve as another assessment of their prior knowledge of geometric terms and concepts and of their understanding of practical applications of geometry.	If you want to use a more formal, paper-and-pencil pre-assessment, I recommend going to the school "archives" and pulling worksheets and pages from old math texts. I like to copy, cut, and paste to create pre- and post-assessments. That way I can customize them to focus on specific goals without having to reinvent the wheel.

LESSON 2	Points, Lines, Line Segments, and Rays	(1 class period)

LESSON SEQUENCE AND DESCRIPTION	TEACHER COMMENTARY
Discussion of definitions and examples. Present definitions and examples of points, line segments, rays, and lines (perpendicular, intersecting, and parallel). Then ask the class to find examples of each around the classroom. Try doing this in a brainstorming format or as an "I Spy" game. Ask students: How does the vocabulary of geometry help us describe the world around us?	This material was a review for most of my students, although specific vocabulary words like *ray, perpendicular,* and *parallel* were familiar but not always mastered. My emphasis here was on identifying the types of lines in the environment—in this case, our classroom. Application of the terms and concepts was the goal.
Small-group problem solving. Put the students in small groups and give each group paper, rulers, markers, Geoboards, and yarn. Write on the board, "The shortest distance between two points is a straight line." Then ask the students to use some or all of their materials to prove that this statement is true. Tell them to plan to share their proof with the class.	I grouped the students randomly for this problem-solving activity because it draws on a variety of skills—visual/spatial skills, creative thinking, abstract thinking, and psychomotor ability. This gave students a chance to be creative in their approach to proving one of geometry's basic rules.
As the groups work, circulate among them, listen to students' thinking, and encourage them to try out their ideas.	A few students needed further clarification to get started, so I used prompts such as, "Select two points on your board. Choose two routes from point to point. Which one is shorter? How do you know?"
Whole-group sharing for lesson closure. Invite the groups to share their proofs. As they do so, probe their thinking: Why did you decide to prove this statement in this way? What other ways did you consider? What did you learn from doing this?	This gave students a chance to hear one another's thinking. Whole-group sharing is a good way to encourage students to learn from (and teach) each other.

LESSON 3	Angles	(2–3 class periods)

LESSON SEQUENCE AND DESCRIPTION	TEACHER COMMENTARY
Discussion of the types of angles and demonstration of angle measurement. On the board, present definitions and examples of angles and the types of angles (right, acute, and obtuse). Then model how to use a protractor to measure angles.	Protractor use is usually taught at higher grades, but I find that my students enjoy the challenge. I used a 15-inch wooden protractor in this

LESSON SEQUENCE AND DESCRIPTION	TEACHER COMMENTARY
Have students work in pairs to find and identify angles in uppercase alphabet letters. As a class, discuss the types of angles that they find.	demonstration, the goal of which was to help students understand the concepts of 90 degrees and angles of less than and greater than 90 degrees, and the terms *right, acute* and *obtuse*. With students who had a limited understanding of large numbers, I discussed the angles in a square. These students compared other angles to square angles in terms of size rather than number of degrees: "Is it smaller than or larger than an angle in a square?"
Practice identifying and measuring angles in small, mixed-readiness groups. Break the class up into small, mixed-readiness groups and give each group protractors and analog clocks (small cardboard practice clocks are good for this). Ask students to identify and measure angles formed by the clock hands at different times. Have each group record their findings on a chart with three columns: *Time, Type of Angle,* and *Measurement.*	It was very helpful to have a parent volunteer to assist me with this activity. One adult for each small group is ideal to ensure that all the students are using the protractors correctly. (It's always easier to make sure a skill is learned correctly the first time than to reteach one learned incorrectly.) If parent volunteers are unavailable, I often rely on students to serve as group leaders. Prior to beginning an activity, I select a student from each group to teach others how to do the activity. When using this strategy, I usually group the most struggling learners together so that I can work more closely with them. In this way, students in the other, mixed-readiness groups are invited to learn from one another, while I can ensure that my most struggling learners are getting what they need with me.
Tiered assignment based on readiness. Assign students to one of three tasks based on readiness levels. All three tasks ask students to distinguish the three types of angles studied and to demonstrate their understanding in written or visual form.	I wanted to give students an opportunity to solidify what they had learned about the types of angles. Tiered assignments allow everyone to work on the same objective but in ways that are appropriate to a variety of instructional levels.

LESSON SEQUENCE AND DESCRIPTION	TEACHER COMMENTARY
Pass out color-coded task cards with the appropriate degree of challenge.	When I use color coding with tiered assignments and assessments, I'm careful to note each task/level/color code in my planning book and change colors for different lessons so that my students do not begin to see themselves as "red" or "blue."
Level 1 Task (Struggling Students) Make a poster showing the three types of angles we discussed: right, acute, and obtuse. Draw and label an example of each type. Then look through magazines and catalogs to find at least two examples of each type of angle and add the pictures to your poster. Your poster should teach us about the types of angles!	This task is for students who struggle with written assignments. I decided posters would give me the information about understanding that I needed without causing these students undue frustration. The magazine pictures they chose told me whether or not they could apply their knowledge to objects outside of the classroom.
Level 2 Task (On-Target Students) Compose a story or poem about angles. You must use all three types of angles that we have talked about. Be sure your story or poem includes the distinguishing characteristics of the type of angles and clearly teaches us about angles. Illustrate a cover page for your story or poem.	This task is aimed at students who have grade-level knowledge and skills about this topic and can express their ideas in writing. The illustration adds a visual dimension to the assignment and may thus support visual learners or students whose writing would be clarified by illustration.
Level 3 Task (Advanced Students) Design and draw a building that has no right angles. Write three paragraphs describing your building and its angles. In your description, include what the building would be used for. What will the doors and windows be like in your building? Will your design be popular with the general public? Why or why not?	This task is designed to give advanced learners a challenge. It encourages them to be creative and flexible, gives them an opportunity to evaluate their ideas in terms of general audience acceptance, and ensures clarity about types of angles.
Discussion for lesson closure. Display the students' work in the classroom for all to see. Lead a whole-group discussion about angles: Are angles important? Why? How do the structures around us reflect the importance of understanding angles? What would our world be like if there was only one type of angle? Would you like it better that way? Why? How does understanding angles help you to describe your environment?	

LESSON 4	Circles	*(1–2 class periods)*

LESSON SEQUENCE AND DESCRIPTION	TEACHER COMMENTARY
Reading assignment on circles and discussion. Read the students a book about circles. Choices might include *What Is Round?* by Rebecca Kai Dotlich, *The Missing Piece Meets The Big O* by Shel Silverstein, or *Round & Round & Round* by Tana Hoban.	I used the book to begin a group discussion about circles.
Ask students to brainstorm a list of places where we see circles. Place the list on chart paper to be posted on the wall.	The list of circles in the world around us that the class came up with included circles from the classroom, their homes, the playground, and so forth. My students were very familiar with circles!
Discuss parts of the circle: radius, diameter, chord, and circumference.	My aim here was to expose the class to the vocabulary of circles.
Partner discussions of circles. Have students work in self-selected pairs to discuss these terms and their use. Ask: How do these new terms help us describe our enviornment? When are these important? Can you think of a time when you might need to know diameter? Circumference? After a few minutes, bring the students back together as a whole group to share their thinking.	I allowed the students to choose their partners for this short activity, as doing so can allow for greater risk-taking in thinking. Also, I knew that the next portion of the lesson would be "teacher choice," and I wanted to make sure to provide some "student choice" along the way.
Journal prompts differentiated by readiness. Print these prompts on color-coded cards so that you can distribute them to students easily.	
Level 1 Prompt (Struggling Students) Make a list of all the places you see circles in your environment (at your home or at school). Be sure to add to the list created by the class. What new ideas can you come up with? Which circle is the most important in your life? Why do you think so?	The first prompt is appropriate for students who struggle to write or who are more concrete and literal thinkers. It asks them to find examples in real-life objects and to evaluate and support their opinions.
Level 2 Prompt (On-Target Students) Imagine that you wake up one morning to a world without any circles. Think about all the things that would be different. Write about how this lack of circles would change your life. Write as many things as you can think of.	The second prompt is less concrete and requires more imaginative responses. It's designed for students who are comfortable with writing three or four paragraphs and who can work with hypothetical situations.

LESSON SEQUENCE AND DESCRIPTION	TEACHER COMMENTARY
Discussion for lesson closure. When the students have completed their writing, lead a whole-group discussion by posing the following question: "What is the one thing you would say about circles to someone who knows nothing about them?" Lead students to consider the importance of circles in our world.	This whole-group discussion gave me a chance to hear what the students had come to know and understand about circles. I took notes about their responses so that I could use the discussion as anecdotal evidence of the students' progress. I also wanted the students to build on their understanding of geometry (see the Unit Objectives, page 97).

LESSON 5 Polygons *(1 class period)*

LESSON SEQUENCE AND DESCRIPTION	TEACHER COMMENTARY
Discussion of the prefixes, names, and attributes of polygons. This lesson focuses on plane figures and the vocabulary related to them. Begin by writing the word *polygon* on the board. Discuss the meaning of the prefix *poly-* (many) and the root *gon* (sides). Put several *poly* words on the board (e.g., *polysyllable, polyvinyl, polygraph, polyester, polyphonic, polytechnical*). What do students think these words mean? Next, write the word *octopus* on the board. Ask students what they know about an octopus. When the response, "It has eight arms," is given, write the word *octagon*. Remind students that the root *gon* means sides. What would the word *octagon* mean? (Other words you may want to look at are *October, octet,* and *octave*.)	I like to incorporate word studies in all subject areas, especially when introducing new vocabulary. Pointing out prefixes, suffixes, and roots helps to build word attack skills. Some students automatically transfer meaning from familiar words to unknown ones having similar prefixes or roots. Other students benefit from being walked through this transfer process and having repeated practice.
Discuss meanings of the words *hexagon* and *pentagon*. Have students look at the word *triangle* and talk about the suffix and root in relationship to the word's meaning.	After going over these words on the board, I made a chart of words having similar prefixes and roots. I displayed the chart on the wall to remind the class of the meanings of the math terms we were learning and also to expand their general vocabulary. Students were encouraged to add other examples throughout the unit.
Geoboard activity. After discussing the names of several polygons, give each student a Geoboard and yarn. (If Geoboards are not available, popsicle sticks, glue, and construction paper will work. Note, however, that if you use popsicle sticks, the shapes will be more similar, due to the sticks' standard length.)	

LESSON SEQUENCE AND DESCRIPTION	TEACHER COMMENTARY
Have the students make figures with given numbers of sides as you call them out (for example, four-sided or seven-sided). Ask students to hold up their shapes for the class to see. Let them talk about how the shapes differ from one another. Point out that some shapes are "regular" (having sides all the same length) while others are "irregular."	In discussing the shapes that the students were making, I made sure to point out that shapes can look different and still be called a triangle, or rectangle, or pentagon.
Ask: Is your shape regular or irregular? How do you know?	
In talking about the students' Geoboard shapes, introduce the term *vertex/vertices*. ("This is where your sides meet.") Also, discuss the number of angles in their polygons.	As students built their polygons, I worked with individuals and small groups as needed to reinforce the ideas of sides of shapes and different numbers of sides. We talked about shapes in the room around us and drew or traced shapes to further understanding and reinforce unit concepts.
When the students can make polygons with different numbers of sides, ask the students to make a polygon of their choice. Use the shapes the students made to discuss: Which two polygons can go together? Why? Are there any others that can go in that group? Why not? What group can we make for them? What can we call our groups?	Here, I wanted the students to classify polygons and describe rules for grouping. I started out with obvious categories like triangles/not triangles. Then I progressed to more subtle differences such as right angles/no right angles. I made sure to point out that grouping polygons would help them understand their similarities and differences.
Have students analyze the groupings and write a statement summarizing each category. Have students share their summaries. Repeat with different categories.	
Discussion for lesson closure. Have the students think of favorite objects. Ask: What polygon is your favorite object most like? What different polygons does it include? How would this object be different if it were shaped like another polygon? Would you like it as well? Why? What is the relationship between structure and function?	I try to ask questions at the end of lessons that invite my students to relate personally to the materials we have worked with. I find that this simple and quick reflection helps them retain information.

LESSON 6	**Tangrams**	*(2–3 class periods)*

LESSON SEQUENCE AND DESCRIPTION	TEACHER COMMENTARY
Presentation of basic tangram shapes. Describe tangrams and show examples of the seven basic shapes. Students should identify triangles, squares, and parallelograms. Demonstrate how the shapes can be used to make other shapes.	Work with tangrams gives students experience with plane figures, helps develop their spatial awareness, and furthers their understanding of parts and whole. I used an overhead projector to introduce the seven basic tangram shapes.

LESSON SEQUENCE AND DESCRIPTION	TEACHER COMMENTARY
	(We had looked at all but the parallelogram in the previous lesson.) I took the opportunity to remind them what the word *parallel* means and to point out how it applied to this polygon. I demonstrated how two triangles can fit together to make one larger triangle, how the square and two small triangles can make a rectangle, and how all seven pieces go together to make a large square.
Reading and discussion of *Grandfather Tang's Story*. Read aloud this book by Ann Tompert. (Another option is *Four Pigs, One Wolf, and Seven Magic Shapes* by Grace Maccarone.) As you read, ask students to point out tangram shapes that they notice in the pictures.	This book illustrates how the pieces can be used to make animal shapes.
Tiered tangram activities based on readiness. Assign students to one of two tiered activities based on their previous grasp of polygons and distribute color-coded activity lists, tangram pieces, and **Differentiated Tangram Tally Sheets** (see Sample 4.2, beginning on page 121), where they will keep track of the different shapes they successfully make with their seven tangram pieces. Be sure to tell the students that they must do the first task on their list first, but that after they complete that one, they can work on the other tasks in any order they would like. *Level 1 Activities (On-Target Students)* 1. Cut out your tangrams and fill out the Tangram Tally Sheet. 2. Choose two of your tangram pieces. Use a Venn diagram to compare and contrast the two pieces. 3. Make a chart classifying your tangram pieces by number of sides, vertices, and angles. 4. Make three new shapes with your tangram pieces. What objects or animals do they look like to you? *Level 2 Activities (Advanced Students)* 1. Cut out your tangrams and fill out the Tangram Tally Sheet. 2. Classify your shapes using your own categories. Explain why each shape belongs in the category to which you assigned it.	My goals with these activities were to provide students with the opportunity to compare, contrast, and classify polygons and give them a chance to work with both visual thinking and creative thinking. The more advanced Tangram Tally Sheet (Level 2) requires students to come up with a greater number of ways to create polygons using a maximum of five tangrams rather than four. The Level 1 activities are less complex and less open-ended than the Level 2 activities. In addition, the tasks on the Level 2 list require greater abstract thought and skill with writing. As I handed out the activity sheets, I explained to students that I would be evaluating them based on the completeness of their work, their time management, and their ability to work cooperatively. I find that letting students in on what I'm actually looking for in their work results in better-quality work.

LESSON SEQUENCE AND DESCRIPTION	TEACHER COMMENTARY
3. What would these polygons look like as three-dimensional shapes? Draw a picture of them. What would they be called? Where might you see these shapes? 4. How many animals from *Grandfather Tang's Story* can you make using your shapes? Can you make other animals or objects? Draw outlines of your figures and share them with a partner. *Note:* Students may work individually or in pairs on these activities. Partners should work with like-colored activity lists, tangrams, and tally sheets.	As the students worked, I moved among them asking questions, providing feedback, and noting when students struggled with their work or finished it with ease. My observations informed my grouping decisions for the remainder of the unit.
Product sharing and discussion for lesson closure. Allow the students to share their work from their activity lists. Ask: What do you like about working with tangrams? What is difficult about it? What did you learn about polygons today? Do polygons have structure?	

LESSON 7   Symmetry and Congruence   *(1–2 class periods)*

LESSON SEQUENCE AND DESCRIPTION	TEACHER COMMENTARY
Discussion of and practice with finding lines of symmetry in classroom objects and in the alphabet. Discuss the meaning of *symmetrical*: "Even distribution—corresponding in size, shape, and position—of parts that are on the opposite side of a dividing or center line."	
Demonstrate a test for symmetry by dividing geometric shapes in half. Ask: Are the two sides the same?	I found that several demonstrations of finding lines of symmetry were necessary. I folded large paper shapes: circles, squares, rectangles, and stars. I drew magic marker lines to divide pictures in two parts.
Discuss symmetry in our environment by showing pictures of flowers, snowflakes, and human faces. Have students tell whether they, themselves, have lines of symmetry. How many lines of symmetry do they have? Can they identify additional lines of symmetry in objects in the classroom?	
Draw lines of symmetry in alphabet letters. Introduce the term *asymmetrical*. Ask: Which letters are asymmetrical?	I found it beneficial to cut large letters out of construction paper so the students could see them folded in half. Actually *folding* letters seemed to help students understand the concept better than just drawing lines. I also demonstrated symmetry using a mirror. Anything to help my students see it!

LESSON SEQUENCE AND DESCRIPTION	TEACHER COMMENTARY
Ask each student to write his or her name using all uppercase letters and then draw lines of symmetry for each letter. Then have the students draw lines of symmetry for the lowercase letters in their names. Be sure to offer assistance as needed.	This activity provided some quick independent practice with identifying symmetrical shapes and lines of symmetry.
Small-group practice with polygon symmetry. Provide a number of envelopes containing paper polygon shapes. Let students work together in random groups to find lines of symmetry for each shape. Have one student per group record their findings, writing the name of each polygon and how many lines of symmetry it has. Next, the groups will brainstorm and list things in nature that are symmetrical. When the groups have completed their work, invite them to share their ideas with the large group. How many lines of symmetry does a square have? How do you know? Where can we find symmetry in nature? What does symmetry tell us about the structure of things around us?	Having the opportunity to handle and fold the shapes helped solidify the students' understanding of lines of symmetry. Some groups stopped when they found one line of symmetry and needed my encouragement to look for more than one.
Introduction of congruent shapes using Geoboards. Introduce the term *congruent* and demonstrate how to tell if shapes are congruent. Be sure to place congruent shapes in different positions as you demonstrate and stress that it is the *size and shape* that must be the same, *not* the position.	Rotating and flipping shapes makes the task harder. I wanted to make sure that the students could identify congruent shapes in different positions.
Have students work in pairs with Geoboards. One student will make a shape on his or her board, and the other will then make a shape that is congruent.	My students enjoy the opportunity to "play" with new information and skills. It helps them understand ideas more fully.
Exit card activity for lesson closure. Tell the students that in order to leave the classroom at the end of the lesson, they will need to create and turn in an "exit ticket" that explains the meanings of *symmetrical* and *congruent*. Distribute index cards and tell students that they may either draw or write their explanations.	Exit cards provide a quick way to assess student understanding. If I find that some students are not able to explain the meanings of the terms, either in pictures or words, then I go back and reteach the terms in a small group.

LESSON 8   Observing and Describing Geometry in Flags   *(1–2 class periods)*

LESSON SEQUENCE AND DESCRIPTION	TEACHER COMMENTARY
Round robin review in mixed-readiness groups. At this point in the unit, students have worked with several geometric terms and shapes. Time for a review!	This review activity got the students up and moving.

LESSON SEQUENCE AND DESCRIPTION	TEACHER COMMENTARY
Place posters on the walls around the room with the following headings (one heading per poster): • Points and lines • Angles • Circles • Polygons • Symmetry • Congruence Working in mixed-readiness groups, the students will rotate from one poster to the next, at two- to three-minute intervals, writing as much as they can about the terms on the posters. When all groups have visited all of the posters, discuss the ideas written on the posters and add to them as needed.	I used mixed-readiness groups to encourage students to share their thinking with one another and learn through the process. I find that this type of review is critical as the students begin to synthesize information late in a unit of study.
Discussion of shapes in state and country flags. Explain that a variety of lines, angles, and plane-figures can be seen in flags of the world. Most flags themselves are usually rectangular in shape. Show several examples of country, state, and nautical flags from books such as *A Pocket Guide to Flags* by Sue Heady, *Flags at Sea* by Timothy Wilson, and *I Know About Flags* by Chris Jaeggi. Most encyclopedias also include a collection of world and nautical flags. Discuss which geometric shapes can be seen in the flags. Flags from the United States, the United Kingdom, Japan, Korea, the Bahamas, Greece, Libya, and Israel are good examples to use. Discuss lines (parallel, perpendicular, and intersecting), types of angles, circles, and polygons. Ask: Which flags have designs that are symmetrical? How can you tell? How does understanding geometry help us describe our environment?	So far in the unit, the students had been identifying and describing points, types of lines, angles, and plane-figures in the classroom environment. During discussions and activities, I had encouraged them to think of places they might see these. Here, I presented them with an idea they might not ordinarily think of in terms of geometric shapes: flags. The students were quite interested in the wide variety of flags. The flag books were very popular items during free time!
Tiered task card activities based on readiness. Give each student one of three color-coded task cards. For each assignment, students must identify and describe geometric shapes in state or country flags.	My goal with this activity was to get the students to synthesize the information we had worked with previously in the unit. I considered differences in writing ability and in abstract thinking skills when designing the three tiers for this activity. At each level, students could draw and color as well as write descriptions.

LESSON SEQUENCE AND DESCRIPTION	TEACHER COMMENTARY
Level 1 Task (Concrete Thinkers) Draw and color your state flag or a flag from another state. List all the geometric shapes that you see. Where do you see examples of parallel, perpendicular, or intersecting lines? Is the flag symmetrical or asymmetrical? Why do you think so? Be specific!	I designed this activity with my most concrete thinkers in mind. These were students who preferred to list information and who might give only "yes/no" answers to questions. Thus, I asked them to give *reasons* for their responses. If needed, I helped these students choose flags incorporating different types of lines.
Level 2 Task (Emerging Abstract Thinkers) Choose two country flags or two state flags. Draw and color each flag. Write a paragraph comparing and contrasting the two flags using the terms *parallel, perpendicular, intersecting,* and other geometric terms. Be sure to discuss the geometric shapes that you see in the two flags. Which flag do you like better? Why?	I created this middle tier for students who were just beginning to think more abstractly. They were also more comfortable with written tasks than were the students I assigned to the Level 1 task.
Level 3 Task (Abstract Thinkers) Imagine that your state has decided to split into two states: For example, East Carolina and West Carolina or North Utah and South Utah. You have been commissioned to design the flags for the two new states. Draw and color the two flags. Write two or three paragraphs discussing your designs. Include in your discussion the geometric features of your designs, the symbolism shown by the geometric features, and how the two flags are alike and different. Be sure your designs include the kinds of shapes, angles, and lines we've studied.	I geared this top tier to my advanced students. These students had shown that they were imaginative and liked to work with hypothetical situations. I had to explain what I meant by symbolism in flag designs, but they quickly caught on and ran with it.
Small- and large-group discussions for lesson closure. Provide time for students to meet in mixed-readiness groups to share their work with one another. Then reassemble as a large group and discuss the use of geometry: Why do you think people who create symbols, such as flags and logos, incorporate ideas about geometry? For example, why do they consider symmetry? Do we like things better when they are symmetrical? Why?	I think it's important for my students to meet in a variety of groupings to share and discuss their work. They all learn from each other.

LESSON 9	**Polyhedrons**	*(1–2 class periods)*

LESSON SEQUENCE AND DESCRIPTION	TEACHER COMMENTARY
Discussion of the attributes of polyhedrons. In this lesson, students will examine three-dimensional figures: cubes, cones, cylinders, pyramids, triangular and rectangular prisms, and spheres.	

LESSON SEQUENCE AND DESCRIPTION	TEACHER COMMENTARY
Write the word *polyhedron* on the board, and explain that *hedron* comes from a root that means *plane* or *face*. Then ask students to think about what they know about the prefix *poly*, and generate some ideas about what *polyhedron* might mean.	I began by reviewing *poly* to see what students had retained from our earlier word study.
Show the class a square and a cube. How are these shapes alike? Different?	Here, I was looking for an understanding of dimension and depth.
Discuss other polyhedrons in terms of their names, number of faces, edges, and vertices. In each case, ask students to brainstorm objects that have the same shape (e.g., box, soup can, ice cream cone). What is the relationship between an object's shape and its function?	As with other lessons in this unit, I emphasized recognition of real-life objects in the environment.
Think–Pair–Share: Is a sphere a polyhedron? Give students two minutes to write their response to this question and their reasons. Then, ask them to turn to a partner and discuss their ideas for the next two minutes. Each partner should express his or her ideas. Finally, pose the question again and have the students discuss their ideas as a large group. Be sure that students have an understanding of the correct answer before moving on.	Think–Pair–Share activities give shy or reluctant students a chance to participate in discussions. I find that they will share their ideas more readily in the larger group after they have "tried them out" during the partner sharing time.
Small-group activity with the vocabulary of polyhedrons. Review the following terms: *face, edge, vertex,* and *base.* Divide the class into random groups of three or four. Give each group a paper bag with a large number on the outside. Inside the bag is one polyhedron.	The students enjoyed this activity, which gave them the opportunity to use the desired vocabulary correctly and to classify the different polyhedrons by various characteristics.
One member of the group places his or her hand in the bag without looking at the shape. That student must not name the shape he or she feels—just describe it to the rest of the small group using the terms *faces, edges, vertices,* and *bases.* Another member of the group will record the group's guess as to the name of the polyhedron based on the description given.	Before they began working, I had a student demonstrate how to describe the shapes without naming them. I found that certain students benefited from having a blindfold when peeking was a temptation.
Rotate the bags among the groups and have students take turns being the "describer." Each group should have a card with bag numbers and their corresponding guesses about the names of the polyhedrons. After all the groups have completed their lists, remove the shapes from the bags, one by one, and check the groups' guesses.	

LESSON SEQUENCE AND DESCRIPTION	TEACHER COMMENTARY
Self-selected application tasks based on Gardner's multiple intelligences. The students will select and complete one of the following tasks:	At this point, I looked back through my unit plans and noticed that I had included a lot of differentiation based on readiness. I wanted also to address learning profiles. I find that Gardner's theory of multiple intelligences is a useful tool for this type of differentiation. I wanted all the students to work with the characteristics and parts of polyhedrons, but I wanted them to be able to do so in ways that were really comfortable for them.
Option 1: Verbal/Linguistic Intelligence Choose two polyhedrons that we have worked with. Write detailed descriptions of each one, including the correct terms: *face, edge, vertex,* and *base.* Your descriptions should enable us to "see" your polyhedrons without having a picture to look at.	
Option 2: Logical/Mathematical Intelligence Create a Venn diagram comparing and contrasting two of the polyhedrons we have worked with. Your diagram should include the following terms: *face, edge, vertex,* and *base.* Create a second Venn diagram using two different polyhedrons.	
Option 3: Kinesthetic Intelligence Using materials provided in the classroom, build models of two of the polyhedrons we have studied. Find a way to label the following on your models: faces, edges, vertices, and bases.	For Option 3, I provided straws, pipe cleaners, cardboard, tape, and other "junk" materials, but I did not tell the students which materials they should use.
Option 4: Visual/Spatial Intelligence Draw detailed diagrams of two of the polyhedrons we have worked with. How will you show all the parts of these polyhedrons (faces, edges, vertices, and bases)? Label the parts.	While students worked on their tasks, I found time to meet with small groups of students based on needs I observed in class and on assessments.
Option 5: Naturalist Intelligence Choose one polyhedron that we have studied. Find and list examples of this polyhedron in nature. Then select one of the objects from your list, draw it, and label the following parts: faces, edges, vertices, and bases.	
Before students begin work on their chosen option, stress that their work must be detailed, neat, and accurate in terms of geometric terminology.	
Product sharing with partners. When the students have finished their work, ask them to share their products with partners who completed different tasks. Tell the students to switch partners a few times so that they get to see a range of products.	This manner of sharing gets the students up and moving, and it gives everyone a chance to share with others. I circulated around the room, offering assistance to those who needed some help sharing their work (either due to language limitations or personality characteristics).

LESSON SEQUENCE AND DESCRIPTION	TEACHER COMMENTARY
3–2–1 exit card activity for lesson closure. Wrap up the lesson by having students complete a 3–2–1 activity on index cards to be turned in and discussed at the start of the next lesson. The students will write the following on their cards: • Three things in nature that are shaped like common polyhedrons. • Two ways to identify a specific polyhedron. • One important use of polyhedrons.	This activity was a quick way to get some closure and invite some more thinking about unit generalization. It was also a good foundation for the next lesson and provided me with useful assessment information.

LESSON 10 **Review and Application** *(2–3 class periods)*

LESSON SEQUENCE AND DESCRIPTION	TEACHER COMMENTARY
Polyhedron review. Begin with a review of the previous lesson, reading ideas from the students' 3–2–1 exit cards. Ask: What other polyhedrons do we see in nature? Can you think of other examples? What's the best way to tell which polyhedron you have? Can you think of any other important uses of polyhedrons? Do polyhedrons have a common structure?	I like to use the students' ideas whenever possible. This can be very validating for students who don't often get to hear their ideas repeated for the class.
Geometry scavenger hunt in mixed-readiness groups. By now, the students have explored points; perpendicular, parallel, and intersecting lines; right, acute, and obtuse angles; circles and their parts; and polygons and polyhedrons. Many of the discussions about these concepts have focused on application to the classroom environment. Now it's time to help students put it all together by transferring their learning to settings outside of the classroom through a scavenger hunt.	I wanted to give students a fun way to apply their understanding of geometry to another setting. Please note that this was not a competitive scavenger hunt!
Set up mixed-readiness groups and give each group a chart so that they can track their progress during the hunt. On the chart, provide a list of the geometric lines, angles, and shapes that you want the students to find, as well as spaces for them to list the objects having the shapes and the locations of the objects.	I chose mixed-readiness groups because I wanted the students to learn from one another. I encouraged each group to find all of the shapes listed, and I allowed groups who finished early to help other students.
Lead the class, charts in hand, around the school and the surrounding grounds. Upon returning to the classroom, each group will share its findings with the large group. Pose questions to focus the discussion. For example: In how many different places did we see parallel lines? Obtuse angles? Using the vocabulary of geometry, what can we say about the structure of architecture? Of nature?	The playground was a good place to start because the students were so active and animated in their search. One group recommended that we expand our hunt to the nature trail, which proved to be a good source of "environmental" geometry.

LESSON SEQUENCE AND DESCRIPTION	TEACHER COMMENTARY
	We stayed together in the same general area, but the groups spread out as much as they could. The summary discussion afterward reined the students back in and prepared them for the RAFT activities coming next.
Self-selected RAFT activities based on interest and learning style. Distribute the **Geometry RAFT Activity Options** (see Sample 4.3, page 123). Tell the students to choose and complete one *Role* with its accompanying *Audience, Format,* and *Topic.* They may work individually or with a partner. Upon completion of the products, the students will share them with the large group. Invite the students to ask one another questions about each other's work. Ask: How do the various products reflect the unit generalizations? What do students like best about their own work? What might they do differently next time?	My students are more motivated when they can choose from a variety of approaches and formats to express what they have come to understand during a unit of study. RAFT activities let them select areas of interest and demonstrate competency in ways that are suited to their individual learning styles. Because so many interests are addressed in the RAFT, I did not use it as part of the assessment for this unit. Rather, I wanted the students to have a chance to focus on an interest area and "stretch their creative muscles."

LESSON 11   Unit Assessment   *(1–2 class periods)*

LESSON SEQUENCE AND DESCRIPTION	TEACHER COMMENTARY
Self-selected final products based on student interest and learning style. The assessment for this unit accommodates individual learning differences. There are two categories of products on the **Geometry Final Product Menu** (see Sample 4.4, page 124); these activities are differentiated based on student interests and learning styles. Students choose one product from each category.	Our unit assessment was a combination of two products. I gave students class time to work on their products so that I could observe their progress and guide and assist them as needed.
Category 1 Product Options Choices include a poster showing labeled examples of geometric shapes; a glossary of geometric terminology; and an illustrated book, *The ABCs of Geometry.*	The first category of products allows students to demonstrate mastery of basic geometry vocabulary and the unit concepts.

LESSON SEQUENCE AND DESCRIPTION	TEACHER COMMENTARY
Category 2 Product Options Choices include a game that teaches geometry concepts (complete with rules and advertising copy); a design and advertisement for a robot that illustrates geometric principles; an illustrated essay about the look of futuristic environments, focused on geometric elements; and a research report on geodesic dome buildings (complete with an illustration or a model).	Product choices in the second category include more creative options. I designed these activities to assess application and synthesis of the geometric concepts.
After students have had time to review and discuss their product options, distribute copies of the **Geometry Final Product Contract** (see Sample 4.5, page 125) for them to sign. Included in the contract is the student's agreement to document and reflect upon his or her work by preparing a **Geometry Final Product Process Log** (see Sample 4.6, page 126).	I find that contracts encourage students' sense of ownership over their products. Process logs invite students to reflect on and evaluate the ways in which they work, and they give me greater insight into students' understanding of their work.
Before students begin work, distribute copies of the **Geometry Final Product Scoring Rubric** (see Sample 4.7, page 127). Explain that they will be turning in self-evaluations when their product is complete.	I based my own evaluations on this same rubric. Overall, I found that the combination of the two products, my observations of and conversations with the students as they worked on those products, and the students' process logs gave me solid information about their mastery of the unit's objectives.

Teacher Reflection on the Unit

The hands-on approach in this unit works well for my students and is a natural fit for the subject matter. Because geometry is such a "physical" part of world, it invites—and I think, demands—the use and exploration of manipulatives. By designing so many of the activities with my students' varying "starting points" in mind, I can ensure that every student has a chance to grow during our study of geometry. Rather than feeling discouraged by the fact that they are working in different groupings at different times, my students like the fact that I consider their needs as I plan my instruction. They also like the fact that many of the unit activities are open-ended enough to allow them some flexibility in their thinking. I feel like this unit, while focusing clearly on my objectives, has a little something for everyone, and because of that, my students find it very engaging.

Elizabeth Hargrave has taught autistic, learning-disabled, and gifted and talented students in grades K–5 in North Carolina. She can be reached at hargravehmnc@aol.com.

SAMPLE 4.1—Geometry Knowledge Rating Scale

Our Knowledge of Geometry

No Knowledge	Little Knowledge	Much Knowledge	Expert Knowledge
(No clue)	*(I've heard of it)*	*(I know it well)*	*(I can teach the class about it)*

SAMPLE 4.2—Differentiated Tangram Tally Sheets

(Level 1)

Directions: Use this grid to keep track of the shapes you make with your tangram pieces. Try to make all of the shapes with different combinations of pieces. Draw a sketch of your shape in the square, outlining its tangram parts.

	Number of Tangram Pieces I Used			
	1	2	3	4
Square				
Rectangle				
Triangle				
Parallelogram				

SAMPLE 4.2—Differentiated Tangram Tally Sheets—*(continued)*

(Level 2)

Directions: Use this grid to keep track of the shapes you make with your tangram pieces. Try to make all of the shapes with different combinations of pieces. Draw a sketch of your shape in the square, outlining its tangram parts.

	Number of Tangram Pieces I Used				
	1	2	3	4	5
Square					
Rectangle					
Triangle					
Parallelogram					

SAMPLE 4.3—Geometry RAFT Activity Options

Role	Audience	Format	Topic
Writer/Illustrator	Kindergarteners	Illustrated children's book	Shapes in My House
Yourself	Our class	Riddles (written or on audio tape)	What Shape Am I?
Songwriter	The world	Song (write and sing)	These Are a Few of My Favorite Shapes
Artist with the Department of Transportation	Drivers	Road signs	New Warning Signs
Jeopardy Host	Contestants	Quiz questions	Shapes for $200
Teacher	3rd graders	Crossword puzzle	Geometric Terms
Poet	The world	Poem	Lines, Circles, or Shapes
Yourself	Our class	Collage	Shapes in Nature

SAMPLE 4.4—Geometry Final Product Menu

Directions: Choose one product activity from each of the following two categories. Select projects that you feel will best demonstrate what you have come to know and understand about geometry during this unit.

Category 1

❏ **Poster.** Using pictures from magazines and newspapers, find and label objects that represent the different types of lines, angles, and shapes that we studied. Include and label parallel, perpendicular, and intersecting lines; right, acute, and obtuse angles; circles; polygons (triangles, squares, rectangles, parallelograms); polyhedrons (pyramids, cones, cylinders, cubes, and rectangular prisms); spheres; and symmetrical and congruent shapes.

❏ **Glossary.** Make a glossary of geometric terms. Define and give an illustrated example of each term. Include line, segment, ray, angles (right, acute, obtuse), circle, radius, diameter, polygon, triangle, square, rectangle, parallelogram, polyhedron, sphere, pyramid, cone, cylinder, cube, rectangular prism, symmetry, congruence, and any other geometric terms that you think should be included.

❏ **Book.** Make a book titled *The ABCs of Geometry*. Try to include a geometric term or concept for each letter of the alphabet (For example: *A* is for *Angle* or *D* is for *Diameter.*) Illustrate your book. Where you can, include as many terms as possible for the letters.

Category 2

❏ **Game.** Invent a game to help teach children about lines, angles, polygons, circles, polyhedrons, congruence, and symmetry. Write a manual for parents and teachers that explains the rules and procedures of the game and discusses the benefits of playing the game. What things will the students who play your game learn about geometry in their world? Write a Saturday morning TV advertisement for your game.

❏ **Geobot.** Design a robot that is made of many different geometric lines, angles, polygons, circles, and polyhedrons. Write three or four paragraphs describing your robot. Include drawings or blueprints of your plans, and tell why you chose to use the shapes you did. Is your robot symmetrical or asymmetrical? Explain why your robot is special and what kinds of things it can do. Write a short advertisement for your robot to put in the Sharper Image catalog.

❏ **Futuristic Community.** Write a one-page essay about life in the year 2200. Describe your environment, especially in terms of the geometric lines, angles, polygons, and polyhedrons you would see. What things will change? What will remain the same and why? Will objects be more or less symmetrical than they are now? Why do you think so? Include a drawing or model of your community of the future.

❏ **Geodesic Dome Buildings.** Research geodesic dome buildings. Draw a picture or build a model of a dome building, and write three or four paragraphs discussing dome buildings. What geometric lines, angles, polygons, and polyhedrons are involved? What are the advantages and disadvantages of geodesic dome buildings? How would your life be different if you lived in a geodesic dome house? Would you like to live in such a house? Why or why not?

SAMPLE 4.5—Geometry Final Product Contract

Name _____ Date _____

These final products give me a chance to demonstrate what I have come to understand about geometry during this unit of study. I have read the unit objectives and have been given opportunities to explore and study the geometric concepts relating to lines, angles, polygons, circles, polyhedrons, symmetry, and congruence.

I have read over the final product options and have selected **two** projects that I feel will best show what I have learned about geometry. I will complete a one-page **Process Log** for *each* product. Each Process Log will include times and dates that I worked on the project, what I feel I learned from working on the product, any problems I encountered, and how I solved those problems. Upon completion of each product, I will evaluate my work using the rubric that my teacher and I have created for my final products.

My selection from the Final Product Menu **Category 1** is

_____

I will have this product and the Process Log completed by _____ (date)

My selection for **Category 2** is

_____

I will have this product and the Process Log completed by _____ (date)

I agree to (check those that apply)

❑ Do my best work on the products and Process Log.
❑ Turn my work in on time.
❑ Work neatly and write legibly.
❑ Use my class time wisely.
❑ Work quietly without disturbing my classmates.
❑ Complete a self-evaluation rubric for each product.
❑ Ask questions when I don't understand something.
❑ Ask for help if I need it.

Signed _____

SAMPLE 4.6—Geometry Final Product Process Log

Name _____ Date _____

Product _____

Dates and times I worked on this product:

Things I learned while working on this product (these should be things you learned about geometry and things you learned about yourself):

Problems I encountered while working on this product and how I solved them:

Things I would do differently next time (and why):

SAMPLE 4.7—Geometry Final Product Scoring Rubric

Name _____ Date _____

Product _____

Level of Achievement	Scoring Criteria
4 Exemplary Achievement	I have gone above and beyond what was required in the following ways: These things are extra-special about my product:
3 Proficient (Expected) Achievement	I have completed my product on time. I have included my *Process Log*. I have done my best work. I have followed the directions, and my work is neat. My product shows that I understand the big ideas and skills of the unit and can apply them.
2 Limited Achievement	I have tried to follow directions, work neatly, and show what I know, but I know this is not my best effort. My product could have been better in the following ways:
1 Minimal Achievement	This product did not get much attention or effort from me. There are many ways I could improve this product. Some of them are listed below:
0 Not Able to Be Scored	I did not complete the assignment.

It's All a Matter of Chance

A Mathematics Unit on Beginning Probability

Unit Developer: Laura C. Massey

Introduction

This four-week mathematics unit is based on the concept of **chance** and guides students to an understanding of the presence of probability in many real-life situations. Students explore random, unpredictable behavior in search of **patterns** to help determine the chances that an event will occur. The application of mathematical problem solving leads students to conclude that we cannot control random events; however, we can predict an outcome as more or less likely to occur.

The unit begins by introducing students to basic probability concepts and relating the concepts to the students' prior knowledge and experience before asking them to make new applications. Then, the students conduct a series of experiments that require them to collect data, critically analyze results, and generate conclusions regarding the likelihood of independent events. With each lesson, students work with greater sample spaces and more in-depth challenges, relying on problem solving and deductive thinking to find probabilities.

After a clear understanding of independent events is established, the unit shifts to the study of dependent events. The students manipulate materials in order to form conclusions about combinations and permutations. Students discover formulas and methods for determining probability using authentic problems. Many of the activities include strategy building and critical analysis so that students can begin developing metacognitive skills.

A major focus of the unit is data collection and presentation using graphs, charts, and tables. The students learn the importance of accuracy and how to most effectively share results. They discuss sampling and experience ways to draw conclusions based on what information is provided. The students transform numbers to fractions, decimals, and percentages to represent the values of probability. In addition, they reflect on their experiences through writing assignments. This allows the students to reflect on their mathematical processes and provides a way to assess their understanding of probability.

Teacher Reflection on Designing the Unit

Probability is one of my favorite areas of math. Teaching concepts related to probability often involves exploratory games and experiments, which are engaging learning experiences for students. I have found that the interactive discovery learning used in many probability games leads students to a solid understanding of the basic concepts. Although I wanted students to manipulate materials and create their own generalizations, I also wanted to be sure that they could transfer the knowledge gained to other real-life situations. I found it necessary to reflect on the games and relate them to the concepts and generalizations of the unit in order to ensure that students were making these connections.

This unit is structured as a series of lessons that support objectives related to probability; however, it is only a sample of what can be done with probability. Numerous authentic problems and activities can join or replace the lessons in this unit. In the end, the goal is for students to understand and use strategies for determining **chance** in varying situations.

Most of the activities in this unit are differentiated by readiness level. Because I teach a class of heterogeneous students who progress at very different rates, I had to be sure that I created lessons that were appropriate for all learners. I added more challenging tasks for advanced students and created flexible lessons so that I was available for students who needed my assistance. When students have learning challenges that severely inhibit their pace or depth in a math progression, I work with a special education teacher to select the key concepts and skills that are most essential for these learners. In most cases, it is possible for the work of these students to stem from and relate to the key concepts and skills for the particular unit. My goal is to keep these students as integral to the work of the class as possible while still addressing their unique needs. Although readiness was the main focus of my differentiation in this unit, I also made efforts to modify lessons according to learning profile and interest. I provided students with choice when appropriate and allowed them to work in various student groupings.

Mathematics Standards Addressed

- Describe events as likely or unlikely and discuss the degree of likelihood, using such words as *certain, equally likely,* and *impossible.*
- Predict the probability of outcomes of simple experiments and test the predictions.
- Understand that the measure of the likelihood of an event can be represented by a number from zero to one.

- Collect data using observations, surveys, and experiments.
- Represent data using tables and graphs such as line plots, bar graphs, and line graphs.
- Propose and justify conclusions and predictions that are based on data, and design studies to further investigate the conclusions or predictions.

Unit Concepts and Generalizations

Chance, Patterns

- Chance is the occurrence of an event with no apparent cause.
- Chance is random.
- Despite this randomness, we can determine the chance of the occurrence of an event.
- Patterns help us determine chances.
- We can predict the occurrence of a single event by the number of possible outcomes.

Unit Objectives

As a result of this unit, the students will *know*

- Dependent and independent events.
- Equivalent fractions, decimals, and percentages.
- Data collection methods, including tallying and sampling.
- Factorial notation.
- Permutations versus combinations.
- Tree diagrams.
- Vocabulary related to the language of probability (*likely, probable, absolute*) as well as *outcome, prediction, experiment, sample space,* and *likelihood.*

As a result of this unit, the students will *understand that*

- Probability refers to the chance or likelihood of an occurrence or event.
- We can determine the probability of an event through mathematical problem solving.
- Probability is based on the number of possible outcomes for a single event.
- The probability of independent events is based on the number of distinct outcomes, and the probability of dependent events is based on the number of possibilities.
- We can predict future outcomes by understanding the probability of the occurrence of a single event.
- A greater number of trials increases the accuracy of our prediction of probability (the Law of Large Numbers).

As a result of this unit, the students will *be able to*
- Determine the probability of a single event.
- Determine the number of outcomes for a single event.
- Make predictions.
- Collect data.
- Express data as fractions, decimals, and percentages.
- Organize data into tables and graphs.
- Interpret and draw conclusions.
- Analyze patterns and trends.
- Relate the concept of chance to real-life situations.
- Apply factorial notation.
- Create tree diagrams.
- Work cooperatively to solve problems.

Instructional Strategies Used
- Brainstorming
- Cooperative problem-solving activities
- Differentiated writing prompts
- Discovery-based activities
- Gardner's multiple intelligences
- Group discussions
- Jigsaw
- Metacognition
- Pre-assessment
- Think–Pair–Share
- Tiered assignments

Sample Supporting Materials Provided

Sample #	Title	Page
5.1	Unit Pre-Assessment	152
5.2	Mathematics Self-Assessment	153
5.3	Generalizations About Chance Homework Assignment	154
5.4	Creating a Character Worksheet	155
5.5	Super Solver Problems	156

Unit Overview

LESSON	WHOLE-CLASS COMPONENTS	DIFFERENTIATED COMPONENTS
LESSON 1 **Introduction and Pre-Assessment** *2 class periods*	Group activity and class discussion of **chance** *20 minutes*	
	Pre-assessment *20 minutes*	
	Introduction to unit concepts and generalizations *10 minutes*	
		Homework assignment based on student interest
	Sharing of homework in small groups *5 minutes*	
	Review of unit generalizations and discussion of homework examples *20 minutes*	
	Creation of Chance Charts and partner activity *30 minutes*	
	Wrap-up review *5 minutes*	
LESSON 2 **Penny Flip** *1 class period*	Introduction to the basic concepts of probability and completion of the penny flip experiment *50 minutes*	Individual questions/supports tailored to student readiness levels
		Homework assignment based on readiness
LESSON 3 **Spinners** *1 class period*	Sharing of homework *5 minutes*	
		Spinner experimentation, data collection, and data representation based on readiness *30 minutes*

LESSON	WHOLE-CLASS COMPONENTS	DIFFERENTIATED COMPONENTS
	Class discussion of results and data analysis *15 minutes*	
		Homework assignment based on readiness
LESSON 4 **A Roll of the Die** *1 class period*	Sharing of homework in pairs *10 minutes*	
	Exploration of the Law of Large Numbers *40 minutes*	
		Self-selected homework assignment based on student interest
LESSON 5 **A Race to the End** *2 class periods*	Review of unit generalizations related to **chance** *5 minutes*	
	Class simulation to explore more complex probabilities *30–45 minutes*	
		Self-selected application activities based on Gardner's multiple intelligences and other learning profile preferences *50–75 minutes*
	Product sharing *20 minutes*	
LESSON 6 **Sampling: Probability Applied** *2 class periods*	Review of unit concepts and generalizations *10 minutes*	
		Tiered assignments based on readiness *40–50 minutes*
	Sharing of results and conclusions in Jigsaw groups *20–30 minutes*	

LESSON	WHOLE-CLASS COMPONENTS	DIFFERENTIATED COMPONENTS
LESSON 7 **Creating a Character** *1 class period*	Art activity to explore combinations *25 minutes* Introduction to tree diagrams *20 minutes* Class discussion of applications *5 minutes*	Anchor activities for students who finish early Tree diagram tiered homework assignment based on readiness
LESSON 8 **So Many Choices** *1 class period*	Sharing of homework products *10 minutes* Exploration of permutations *20 minutes* Think–Pair–Share to discuss predictions and processes *10 minutes* Class discussion of factorial notation *10 minutes*	
LESSON 9 **Permutations** *1 class period*	Class discussion of independent events, combinations, and permutations *10 minutes*	Tiered independent activity based on readiness and learning profile *30–40 minutes* Anchor activity for students who finish early
LESSON 10 **Final Assessment** *2 class periods*		Formal assessment of understanding and skill based on readiness *1 class period* Self-selected project based on interest and learning preference *1 class period*

LESSON	WHOLE-CLASS COMPONENTS	DIFFERENTIATED COMPONENTS
LESSON 11 **Closure and Celebration** *1 class period*	Sharing of student projects and further exploration of games *50 minutes*	

Differentiated Homework Assignments

Throughout this unit, students are provided with homework assignments appropriate to their differing interests and readiness levels. Some are self-selected; most are teacher-assigned. These assignments, usually based on specific prompts, allow students to explore ideas and skills related to probability in ways that engage them and provide an appropriate degree of challenge to thinking. All of the differentiated homework assignments in this unit encourage students to see and reflect on the presence of probability in their own lives and stretch their thinking beyond the classroom.

Teacher Reflection on the Use of Differentiated Homework Assignments

It makes little sense to me to differentiate activities within the classroom only to send my students home to work on the same assignments regardless of their differing levels of understanding and skill and their varied interests. Therefore, during the planning stages of this unit, I considered how I might provide homework assignments that required all of my students to work with my "non-negotiables" (the unit objectives) and yet respected those students' many differences. I also wanted to vary teacher and student choice with regard to homework. Thus, I looked for ways to encourage my students to apply their own interests to what we were discovering during class and for ways that they could work at varied skill levels.

I also made sure to provide time for my students to share their homework with one another. In this way, they realized that they all were working with the unit's important information and skills, and at the same time, they learned a lot about their classmates' interests.

Unit Description and Teacher Commentary

LESSON 1	Introduction and Pre-Assessment	(2 class periods)

LESSON SEQUENCE AND DESCRIPTION	TEACHER COMMENTARY
Note: Prior to the unit, create folders so that each student can keep his or her assignments, activity sheets, journal entries, and other materials together in one place. Distribute these folders before each lesson.	I find that providing folders helps my students to stay better organized. This is especially important for my ADHD and learning-disabled students, who sometimes struggle to keep up with their papers.
Group activity and class discussion of chance. Place the students in small (random) groups and provide each group with a game or activity that is based on **chance** (for example, *Magic 8 Ball, Twister, Chutes and Ladders, UNO, Parcheesi, Candy Land*). Allow time for the groups to explore the games/activities and then bring the class together to debrief. During this discussion, highlight how the outcome of each game/activity is determined by chance. As the students begin to use terms related to probability, record and discuss each one. Ask the students to define chance. Explain that this math unit will address the likeliness of an event occurring.	This was a great "hook" for bringing attention to the subtlety and frequency of probability in our everyday lives. My students were very engaged by the activity, and it led nicely to a discussion of probability. The students shared ideas and insights, and my notes of the debriefing discussion allowed me to informally assess their understanding of chance and probability.
Pre-assessment. Distribute the **Unit Pre-Assessment** (Sample 5.1, page 152) and **Mathematics Self-Assessment** (Sample 5.2, page 153) handouts. Remind students that this is their chance to share their strengths and interests with you and that their responses will help you plan the unit. Give the students time to complete both assessments. Work in a small group with any students needing assistance.	The pre-assessment allowed me to evaluate the students' background knowledge and skills levels. The self-assessment added the students' perspective: their own perceptions of their skills, strengths, weaknesses, and interests in the area of mathematics. Working with students who needed help with completing the assessments gave me a chance to monitor their understanding.
Introduction to unit concepts and generalizations. Present and discuss the five unit generalizations on the overhead and make sure that each student understands the statements.	I also created a list of the unit generalizations on chart paper and kept it posted in the classroom so that we could refer to the generalizations throughout the unit.

LESSON SEQUENCE AND DESCRIPTION	TEACHER COMMENTARY
Homework assignment based on student interest. Distribute copies of the **Generalizations About Chance Homework Assignment** (see Sample 5.3, page 154) and ask students to come up with at least three examples of real-life occurrences that would fit under each unit generalization.	This assignment requires students to make personal connections with the unit's big ideas. I wanted my students to see that the unit generalizations related not only to math, but also to other disciplines and situations. I provided struggling students with examples for each generalization to get them started.
Sharing of homework in small groups. Place students in random groups of three and give the groups five minutes to share their ideas from the homework assignment.	I find that having students first share their ideas in small groups enhances whole-group discussion.
Review of unit generalizations and discussion of homework examples. Next, lead a whole-group discussion of examples related to the generalizations. Write students' ideas on the chart paper and highlight the variety of situations in which probability and **chance** might arise.	During the whole-group discussion, I listened for students' varying levels of understanding and ability to apply their understanding to real-life events.
Creation of Chance Charts and partner activity. Distribute a piece of construction paper to each student and tell the students to turn the paper horizontally and draw a horizontal line near the top of the paper. Each student should create a continuum by drawing five points on the line at equal intervals. One end of the line should indicate "no chance." The other end should indicate "definite chance." Draw an example on the board.	One of my primary goals for this unit was for students to see that math is all around them. This activity addressed that goal directly. The creation of the Chance Charts required the students to work with the concept of **chance** and to use the language of probability.
Refer students to the terms generated in the previous discussion and allow them to choose the terms to place along the continuum.	By choosing their own labels, the students were able to personalize their Chance Charts and use terms that made the most sense to them. Throughout this unit, I encouraged the students to add to their charts, which became important visual tools.
When all students have finished, have them choose partners. Each pair should think of 12 events that might fall at different points along the Chance Charts and write them on small scraps of paper. (For example, "I will live forever," "It will get dark tonight," "Another Harry Potter book will be released.") The students will glue the events along their Chance Charts, and pairs of students should share and compare their charts with others.	I allowed the students to choose their own partners because I hoped this would encourage them to take risks and share unique ideas. Whenever I use partner work in my instruction, I'm careful to watch for problematic pairings, which I monitor closely and coach as necessary.

LESSON SEQUENCE AND DESCRIPTION	TEACHER COMMENTARY
Wrap-up review. Conclude by revisiting the five generalizations and adding new ideas to the lists of examples.	A quick review of our work and discussions.

LESSON 2　　　　**Penny Flip**　　　　*(1 class period)*

LESSON SEQUENCE AND DESCRIPTION	TEACHER COMMENTARY
Note: Post the following vocabulary words at the front of the room and refer to them as needed throughout this lesson: *experiment, prediction, independent events,* and *outcome.*	I wanted these key terms to become part of my students' language.

Introduction to the basic concepts of probability and completion of the penny flip experiment. Write the definition of probability on the board: "Probability is the study of random behavior."

Inform students that they will conduct a coin-tossing experiment that will demonstrate the probability of a coin landing on each side. Explain that the steps used in this experiment will be used in more complex experiments later. Remind the students to follow the directions carefully and to ask questions if something is unclear.

Before beginning the experiment, ask students to predict how many times a penny will land on each side if it is flipped 20 times. Write students' predictions on the board, and ask several students to explain their predictions.

Provide each student with a penny and a sheet of graph paper. Tell the students to flip the penny 20 times and record the results. You may have to help some students find a way to record their data (for example, using tally marks).

Ask the students to share what happened during the experiment. Were their predictions accurate? Why or why not? Using your own results, create a bar graph on the overhead. Point out the importance of labeling each axis, scaling the numbers appropriately, and including a descriptive title.

Tell the students to make their own graphs following the same procedure and using their own data.

When the graphs are complete, ask the students to make true statements based on them (for example, "The coin landed on tails more than heads.").

I chose to have a group discussion here for two reasons. First, I was still assessing the students' level of prior understanding, which I did by making notes during the discussion. Second, I was laying the foundation for the rest of the unit. This lesson involves making predictions; conducting an experiment; recording and graphing data; and reviewing fractions, decimals, and percentages. Because I knew we would be repeating this process throughout the unit, I needed to make sure my students could use these skills.

During the experimentation, I circulated throughout the room posing questions of varying levels to probe students' thinking and encourage them to think about the implications of our experiment. I asked some students questions such as, "How many times would you expect the coin to land on heads if it were tossed 100 times?" Other students were ready for more abstract questions, such as, "Will results always show an equal number of heads and tails? Should they?"

LESSON SEQUENCE AND DESCRIPTION	TEACHER COMMENTARY
Introduce the idea that probability can be expressed as a fraction, decimal, or percent. (For example, a penny has a 1/2, a 0.5, or 50% chance of landing on heads.) Have students fill in these numbers on their Chance Charts. Ask: Where should each fraction, decimal, or percent be placed on the charts? Conclude this lesson by asking the class whether they could control the results of the experiment. Ask: Were you able to predict your results? How did you make your predictions? Were the results random? Why would people study "random behavior"? Students should leave the lesson with an understanding that although we cannot control the results, we can make predictions based on the number of possible outcomes.	Here, I wanted the students to really think about our unit generalizations on the way to arriving at a clear generalization statement.
Homework assignment based on readiness. Assign students one of the following writing prompts: *Prompt 1 (Lower Readiness)* Write four statements about the probability of a coin landing on heads. Use fractions, decimals, and percents. *Prompt 2 (Higher Readiness)* Explain the following statement: "Flipping a coin is a fair way to make a decision." *Prompt 3 (Highest Readiness)* If a coin lands on heads the first time it is flipped, what is the probability that it will land on heads the next time? Explain your answer.	While some students needed more practice with fractions, decimals, and percents, others were ready to work with more abstract ideas. Students with more basic IEP goals worked with homework appropriate to those goals. I followed a similar pattern of modifying homework and classwork throughout the unit.

LESSON 3   **Spinners**   *(1 class period)*

LESSON SEQUENCE AND DESCRIPTION	TEACHER COMMENTARY
Note: During this lesson, students use spinners to explore probability. Although manufactured plastic spinners provide the greatest accuracy, students can also make their own.	

LESSON SEQUENCE AND DESCRIPTION	TEACHER COMMENTARY
Sharing of homework. Begin this lesson by inviting students to share their homework assignments. Use the students' writing as a review of information and as an introduction to the concept of "independent events." Student responses to the writing prompts can initiate this brief discussion.	I find that my students develop new understanding more easily when their own ideas are used as a springboard for that understanding.
Spinner experimentation, data collection, and data representation based on readiness. Those students who have a clear understanding of the basic concepts of probability will work on the day's basic task individually and then move on to more complex problems. These students begin with spinner patterns divided into fourths and then move to patterns of different-sized sections (e.g., thirds, eighths, twelfths, or a combination of many). Other students will work with the teacher.	Based on the pre-assessment and on my observations during previous activities, it was clear that some students had prior knowledge of the basic concepts of probability. Because these students did not require preparatory discussions or teacher guidance, I allowed them to move more quickly through a basic task and on to more complex problems in which the sections on the spinners were not equal. Although these students were working with more complex probabilities, they were still required to record and discuss their findings.
On the overhead, display a spinner pattern that splits a circle into fourths, each a different color. Ask questions related to the probability of the different outcomes. Which color do you think the spinner will land on first? Why? If we spin the spinner 10 times, how many times do you think it will land on red? Be sure to have students explain their answers.	
Assign students to pairs and pass out graph paper and a spinner to each pair. Instruct the students to spin the spinner 40 times and record the results on their own papers. Working with their partners, students should transfer their results onto a graph. Refer students to example graphs if guidance is needed.	I created mixed-readiness pairs so that those students who were a bit further along in their understanding of probability could share their knowledge with their partners. However, I was careful not to make the differences between ability too great in each pair, as I find that doing so usually frustrates both students in the pair.
	I identified some students I knew would have difficulty with this task and worked with them as a small group rather than having them work in pairs.
Class discussion of results and data analysis. Bring students together and discuss the results. Be sure to discuss the fraction, decimal, and percent values for the probability of each color on the spinner.	Students chose the type of graph to use to display their results. This allowed them to synthesize the data in a way that made the most sense to them. I provided examples of different types of graphs for students who needed support.

LESSON SEQUENCE AND DESCRIPTION	TEACHER COMMENTARY
At the end of the lesson, have the students add these new values (1/4, 3/4, 0.25, 0.75, 25%, 75%) to their Chance Charts. Compare the probabilities found during this activity with those of the coin-tossing experiment. What determines the probability of an event? Conclude by establishing that the number of possible outcomes determines the likelihood of an event occurring.	The Chance Charts again served as a visual tool for comparing probabilities.
Homework assignment based on readiness. Give each student a spinner pattern that is divided into different sized sections indicating a different color for each. (You can distribute as many different patterns as you like.) The students' task is to develop predictions for the number of outcomes for each color if they spin their spinner 60 times. They must also provide a rationale for the predictions. Give students working at a more advanced level the option of creating an original spinner pattern.	I assigned spinner patterns based on each student's readiness. Students who had a greater understanding of fractions received the most complex patterns (say, a spinner divided into two thirds and two sixths rather than one half and two fourths). I asked students who had already explored this concept during class to construct their own patterns and make predictions about outcomes.

LESSON 4   **A Roll of the Die**   (*1 class period*)

LESSON SEQUENCE AND DESCRIPTION	TEACHER COMMENTARY
Sharing of homework in pairs. Allow time for the students to share their homework assignments from Lesson 3 and to test their predictions with a partner. Circulate as the students are working, and discuss the predictions and results of each experiment. Ask: How might these results differ if you conducted 80 trials? One hundred? Two hundred?	When they shared their homework, I made sure that students were paired with others who had used a spinner pattern of similar difficulty level so all were working with appropriate materials. Where necessary, I also substituted alternate spinner tasks relevant to IEP goals.
Exploration of the Law of Large Numbers. Invite students to share examples of times when they have used a six-sided die. Ask: What are the possible outcomes when rolling a die? Tell the students that you are going to roll a die 30 times. How many times do they predict the die will land on 1? How about on 2? On other numbers? Ask the students to share their predictions and explain their thinking.	This was a great way to get students to work as a whole group to construct the concept of the Law of Large Numbers. In my experience, learning gained from interactive experiences tends to stick with students.

LESSON SEQUENCE AND DESCRIPTION	TEACHER COMMENTARY
Give each student a die. Each student will roll the die 30 times and record the data using tally marks. When they have finished, discuss the results. Did the results match students' predictions? If not, how can we obtain more accurate results? Next, have each student report his or her results and record each on the board. Total the number of rolls for each outcome. Ask the students to explain why compiling the data might provide more accurate results. At this point introduce the Law of Large Numbers. Be sure that everyone understands that the results of the experiment gained greater accuracy (based on theoretical probability) with a greater number of trials. Discuss other examples of when this law would impact experiment results. Conclude the lesson by challenging the students to find the Law of Large Numbers in areas other than math.	As the lesson progressed, the class tested the "rules" of probability together. Everyone's contribution helped lead us to a common goal. The students really enjoyed this collaborative effort. During our discussion, we came up with other situations involving data collection in which the Law of Large Numbers would apply. For example, the life of a typical battery might be overestimated or underestimated if one looked only at the lives of a few batteries rather than at a large number of them. The same might be true for the average height or weight of humans.
✴ **Self-selected homework assignment based on student interest.** Ask students to choose one of the following areas of study and explain a situation in which the Law of Large Numbers would apply to it: science, psychology, athletics, economics, business, or (with teacher approval) another discipline of their choice.	The students chose disciplines based on their interests. I worked with some of my students to help them generate ideas.

LESSON 5	A Race to the End	*(2 class periods)*

LESSON SEQUENCE AND DESCRIPTION	TEACHER COMMENTARY
Review of unit generalizations related to chance. Encourage the students to apply these statements to the activities completed thus far in the unit.	Because we had explored several new concepts by this point in the unit, I thought it was a good time to revisit our generalizations and relate them to our current understandings.

LESSON SEQUENCE AND DESCRIPTION	TEACHER COMMENTARY
Class simulation to explore more complex probabilities. Split the students into two groups. Assign one student in each group to be the dice roller. Assign 12 students in each group to be runners in a race and give them numbers (1–12) to attach to their shirts. (If the numbers do not work out in your class, have students double up on roles.) Explain to both groups that the roller will roll two dice simultaneously. The person whose number is rolled moves forward one step. The first person to the finish line wins. Ask: Who do you predict the winner will be? Who cannot win? Why? Line the runners up on the starting line, and tell the rollers to begin the race.	This kinesthetic activity actively involved the students in the discovery of new concepts. I believe it's important for my students to have opportunities for movement in the classroom. It helps them grasp new ideas and keeps them engaged. This is an activity that works for virtually all learners. Students with physical handicaps can still generally "run" this race.
When the races are over, have students sit in the spots where they finished. On the chalkboard, record how many times each number was rolled. Encourage the students to tell how they felt about the race.	By having the students remain in their positions, I was able to use them as "visual evidence" in our discussions. As we analyzed our experiment, the students' positions represented the results.
Give each student two dice of different colors. Tell the students to list all of the possible combinations for each of the outcomes when rolling two dice. Remind the students that the roll of, say, 3 and 4 is different from a roll of 4 and 3. When finished, ask the students to describe the number of combinations in relation to the results of the game. At the conclusion of this lesson, it should be clear that the greater number of possible combinations for each outcome increases the likelihood of rolling the number.	This next step in the lesson allowed students to work at their own paces and gave me a chance to check in with students whom I suspected needed some guidance and meet with advanced learners to probe and challenge their thinking.
Self-selected application activities based on Gardner's multiple intelligences and other learning profile preferences. Students can work individually, with a partner, or in groups of three on one of the following activities. Directions for each task require students to use mathematical reasoning and the language of probability to complete their products. Option 1: *Verbal/Linguistic Intelligence* You are one of the runners in the race. Write a letter to the coordinator of the race explaining why this race was or was not fair.	I differentiated these tasks based on learning profile. First, the students had the choice of working independently or with other students. Second, they could choose how they would present their understanding of the previous activity and its relationship to probability.

LESSON SEQUENCE AND DESCRIPTION	TEACHER COMMENTARY
Option 2: Visual/Spatial Intelligence Make a chart to display the possible outcomes when rolling two dice. Find a way to prove that the race is either fair or unfair. *Option 3: Logical/Mathematical Intelligence* Develop new rules for the race to make it fair for all participants. Be ready to explain why your rules are better. *Option 4: Interpersonal/Intrapersonal Intelligence* Reenact today's race in your imagination. Include dialogue, inner thoughts, and commentary regarding the fairness of the race.	
Product sharing. Conclude the lesson by providing time for the students to share their task products with one another in pairs or in small groups.	As students shared, I prompted them to consider how knowing about probability helped them judge the fairness of their activities or games.

LESSON 6   **Sampling: Probability Applied**   *(2 class periods)*

LESSON SEQUENCE AND DESCRIPTION	TEACHER COMMENTARY
Review of unit concepts and generalizations. Review the ideas and skills addressed so far in the unit. Explain that the goal of this lesson is to explore probability further by solving a real-life problem.	Because this is the final lesson on independent events, I developed activities that require students to combine and use information in more authentic situations. The goal was for students to see how the rules of probability can be applied to a variety of situations.
Tiered assignments based on readiness. Place the students in similar-readiness groups of no more than four. Assign each group to a separate area of the room and pass out the assignment instructions (written on cards) and materials. The tasks are listed in increasing order of difficulty. *Task 1 (Lower Readiness)* You have told your friend secrets in the past. You figured out that she has told others 9 of the 15 secrets that you shared. Should you tell her another secret? Use probability to explain your answer.	I grouped the students by readiness level because the activities require varying degrees of conceptual understanding. I wanted to ensure that all students were engaged and challenged appropriately. Task 1 provides explicit instructions and the problem directly relates to the concept of probability.

LESSON SEQUENCE AND DESCRIPTION	TEACHER COMMENTARY
Task 2 (Higher Readiness) There are 20 seconds to go in the basketball game and your team is down by 7 points. Your coach has instructed you to foul so the clock will stop. The point guard has made 6 of his last 14 free throws and the center has made 4 of his last 8 free throws. Should you foul the point guard or the center? Use probability to solve the problem and explain your answer.	This task requires students to take greater responsibility in strategic planning to solve a more complex problem.
Task 3 (Highest Readiness) You are trying to raise money for a 5th grade field trip. Your class has decided to sell plain, chocolate, and cream-filled doughnuts to the students at your school, but you do not know how many boxes to order. You'd take a poll, but unfortunately, all classes but the 3rd grade are on a field trip and you need to place your order today. How should you determine how many boxes of doughnuts to order for the entire school? How does this relate to our study of probability?	Here, the students must relate the concept of sampling to probability. This task involves more logical thinking skills and an abstract application of knowledge. Students working with IEP goals that differed from those of the unit had problems that used wording much like one of these three tasks—for example, related to friends, playing basketball, or raising money.
As the students work in their groups, meet with individuals and groups of students as needed to ensure success with the tasks.	This was another opportunity to do some informal assessing, and I took notes as I met with the students. I made sure that all students—regardless of readiness levels—had the opportunity to interact with me one-on-one at various points during the unit.
Sharing of results and conclusions in Jigsaw groups. When the groups have completed their work, place the students in Jigsaw groups to describe their activities and results. Questions for the groups to consider include the following: • What were the steps that your group followed to solve the problem? How does this relate to probability? • How can you apply this knowledge to other situations? • What do you think it means to take a sample from a population? Conclude this lesson by asking groups to share their conclusions about the presence of probability in real-life experiences.	I find that Jigsaw groups help to ensure that everyone has a chance to explain his or her processes. Also, the smaller groups promote better listening and more open discussions. I met with IEP students to talk about how they solved their problems. My main objective here was to get the students to connect personally to our study of probability. All students can participate in discussions about whether or not something is likely or unlikely to happen in their lives.

LESSON SEQUENCE AND DESCRIPTION	TEACHER COMMENTARY
	I injected questions about students' interests, as well as very advanced questions for students whose knowledge on this concept was advancing rapidly.

LESSON 7	**Creating a Character**	*(1 class period)*

LESSON SEQUENCE AND DESCRIPTION	TEACHER COMMENTARY
Note: At this point, the focus of the unit shifts from finding the probability of a single event based on the number of distinct outcomes (independent events) to finding probability based on the number of possibilities (dependent events).	I began this lesson with a whole-group activity because I was introducing a new concept. I wanted to be sure that all of the students had a basic understanding before I began differentiating.
Art activity to explore combinations. Provide each student with nine index cards. Tell the students that they will create flip books of characters.	This activity integrates art into our study of probability.
Each student should draw three heads, three bodies, and three sets of legs on the nine index cards. When the students finish, they should pick up a **Creating a Character Worksheet** (see Sample 5.4, page 155) and begin answering the questions.	While I worked with students needing assistance, I encouraged others to work at their own pace.
Anchor activities for students who finish early. Tell students that when they finish they are to work on one of three activities:	Students chose the anchor activity that appealed most to their individual learning profiles.
1. Write a story about one (or all) of your characters. 2. Continue forming additional body parts for your characters. 3. Create another activity in which you can form different combinations.	
Introduction to tree diagrams. Bring the students together and model the formation of a tree diagram showing all possible characters. Show students how each combination is represented through this visual diagram.	
Have the students choose from one of their rows on the Creating a Character Worksheet and practice creating a tree diagram. Observe and note the students' ability to create tree diagrams.	

LESSON SEQUENCE AND DESCRIPTION	TEACHER COMMENTARY
Refer the students to the table on the worksheet (see Sample 5.4). Tell them that a formula exists for determining the number of combinations based on the number of choices for each body part. Give the students several minutes to work on the problem. Allow those who figure it out to share their thinking with classmates. Practice with a few more examples to assure that all students comprehend how this formula works.	Here, I wanted the students to discover the formula on their own, as discovery often leads to lasting learning.
Class discussion of applications. Conclude this lesson by discussing when it might be important to know how many possible combinations exist.	Again, I wanted the students to see the practical applications of what we were studying.
Tree diagram tiered homework assignment based on readiness. Assign the students to one of the following tasks and instruct them to use tree diagrams to show the different possibilities. *Task 1 (Lower Readiness)* It's early Monday morning and your mother has laid out the following clothing items for you to choose from: a red shirt, a blue shirt, a white shirt, blue jeans, and khaki pants. How many different outfits can you make with the clothes your mother has provided? *Task 2 (Higher Readiness)* You are making cupcakes for a class celebration. Your classmates have indicated that they would like a choice of different cupcakes. You have: chocolate and yellow cake batter; strawberry, white, and caramel icing; and green and blue sprinkles. How many different types of cupcakes can you offer your classmates? (You can draw each cupcake if it helps you to solve the problem.) *Task 3 (Highest Readiness)* You are trying to determine your schedule for next year at Scott Middle School. First period, you can take art, chorus, or band. Second period, you can take technology or creative writing or be an office assistant. Third period you can take a foreign language: German, Spanish, French, or Latin. Figure out how many different schedules are possible based on these options.	I assigned the homework based on student performance throughout the unit and during this particular lesson. Task 1 offers the fewest possible combinations; Task 3, the most. To scaffold this assignment further, I provided laminated cards showing the various clothing items for the students to manipulate.

LESSON 8	So Many Choices	(1 class period)

LESSON SEQUENCE AND DESCRIPTION	TEACHER COMMENTARY
Sharing of homework products. Allow the students time to share and describe the process of creating their tree diagrams. Be sure that a variety of diagrams are presented so that the students can gain more experience with this data-organization strategy.	I like to encourage metacognition and to give my students the opportunity to understand others' perspectives and thought processes.
Exploration of permutations. Give each student four different-colored cubes and crayons. Have students determine and record the different possible combinations when using two, three, and four colored cubes. Circulate through the room to make sure that students are on track. If students finish early, ask them to analyze the strategies they used to find all of the combinations, and encourage them to devise other strategies for determining the number of combinations. Post the following questions on the chalkboard: • What did you do to find all the possible combinations? • Is there another way to find all the possibilities? As a class, review the number of combinations for two, three, and four cubes and record each on the chalkboard.	Students first worked independently on this activity so that they would begin to build a personal understanding of the concept. I also wanted them to explore their own strategies for solving such problems. I found that a few students needed my assistance while others quickly developed efficient strategies for finding the combinations. These students could move on to analyzing their thinking and considering other paths for solving the problem. Meanwhile, I worked with groups of students who needed guidance in developing strategies to solve the problem. I wanted to give as many students as possible a chance to share their thinking. All students benefit from exposure to different methods, and this kind of sharing helps them to see that there is not always one "right" way to solve a problem.
Think–Pair–Share to discuss predictions and processes. Ask students to use the information just reviewed to predict how many combinations are possible when five cubes are used. Give students time to think independently about your questions. Then, have students share their predictions in pairs. Provide each pair with another colored cube so that each pair will have five cubes of different colors. Were your predictions accurate? Why or why not? How do you know?	Think–Pair–Share is a quick and easy way to engage student thinking and get them talking.

LESSON SEQUENCE AND DESCRIPTION	TEACHER COMMENTARY
As the students finish testing their predictions in pairs, place them into groups of four to share and discuss their findings. Provide another colored cube to any groups that finish early, and ask students to figure out how many combinations are possible *now*.	
Class discussion of factorial notation. When all of the students have completed the previous task, discuss the number of combinations that were found based on five cubes. Write the correct answer (120 combinations) on the chalkboard. Ask: Do you notice any **patterns**? Explain that a formula exists for solving such problems and challenge the students to discover it. Guide students to the concept of factorial notation. It is important that you or a student explain the formula clearly. Why does this formula work?	Generating the formula for factorial notation can be difficult for students. I recommend searching for patterns, exploring all operations, and manipulating the cubes. Although not all students will construct this formula, advanced students tend to figure it out. Other students will benefit from witnessing the thought processes of those who generated the formula. I encouraged all students to ask questions to help guide their growing understanding of mathematical thinking.

LESSON 9	**Permutations**	*(1 class period)*

LESSON SEQUENCE AND DESCRIPTION	TEACHER COMMENTARY
Tiered independent activity based on readiness and learning profile. All students will undertake the following task, working on their own. *Task A* Given the letters *A*, *B*, *C*, and *D*, how many possible combinations can be formed? Solve the problem. Then describe the strategy and method that you used to solve the problem. You may use any technique to display your answer (for example, a written description, a diagram, a step-by-step set of directions). Students who have a solid understanding of combinations and permutations and who need additional challenge will *also* undertake the following: *Task B* Describe the major difference between this problem and the type of problem you solved during the Creating a Character activity. Also, explain the formulas that can be used to solve each.	This differentiated activity gave me a chance to assess my students' grasp of the ideas presented in the previous two lessons. It also gave the students a choice in terms of problem-solving strategies and how they might show their answers. I met individually with students as they worked, providing assistance as needed: review, help clarifying thought processes, and extra boosts to push thinking to another level. Because I expected these students would be able to finish Task A quickly, I created an additional task for them to work on.

LESSON SEQUENCE AND DESCRIPTION	TEACHER COMMENTARY
Anchor activity for students who finish early. Tell students that when they finish their work, they should pick up a copy of the **Super Solver Problems** (see Sample 5.5, page 156) and choose a problem to work on and present to their classmates.	The Super Solver Problems are more complex applications of the concept of permutations and are designed for more advanced students.
Class discussion of independent events, combinations, and permutations. Conclude the lesson by reviewing the vocabulary and concepts highlighted in the three previous lessons: independent events, combinations, and permutations. Discuss: How does understanding these things help us to make better predictions?	

LESSON 10	Final Assessment	*(2 class periods)*

LESSON SEQUENCE AND DESCRIPTION	TEACHER COMMENTARY
Note: The final assessment for this unit consists of two parts.	
Formal assessment of understanding and skill based on readiness. The first part of the final assessment is a formal mathematics post-test in which the students complete a set of computation and application problems. Create different forms of the test for varying student readiness levels in the classroom.	The first part of the unit assessment evaluates students' skill levels. It made little sense to me to test all students the same when I had not taught them the same. I designed two different levels of the test based on my previous assessments. Students were tested on the material that they had worked with during the unit and on the instruction that they had received.
Form A (Lower Readiness) The first test form should include questions such as the following: You have a spinner that is half red, one-fourth blue, and one-fourth green. If you spin it eight times, how many times do you predict that you would land on green? Explain your answer. What are the chances that you will draw an ace from a deck of cards? What are the chances that you will draw a face card?	
Form B (Higher Readiness) The second test form should include questions such as the following: A tennis player has won two-thirds of her matches. Based on her previous record, what is the probability that she will lose a match? A drawer contains three pairs of red socks, four pairs of white socks, and one pair of black socks. What are the chances that you will pull out a red sock? How many times will you have to pull from the drawer to get to the point where you have a 50% chance of pulling a red sock?	

LESSON SEQUENCE AND DESCRIPTION	TEACHER COMMENTARY
Self-selected project based on interest and learning preference. The second part of the assessment asks the students to apply their learning to authentic situations that involve probability. Allow them to choose from two options:	Here, students transferred conceptual understanding to "real life"—and chose how they would do so.
Option A Using materials in the classroom or brought from home, create an original game with roles that implement the concepts of probability. Be prepared to show how the game incorporates concepts of probability.	The goal here is to create a game that is clear and original.
Option B There are various stations around the room, each featuring a game, example, or situation in which probability is a factor. Move throughout the classroom and work at all stations. At the end of the period, choose two of the activities and write an explanation for a games magazine of how probability factors into each. Include as much information from the unit of study as possible.	I knew that creating an original game would be too intimidating for some students, so I gave them the option of evaluating examples that already existed. Students with IEP goals that were very different from this unit's goals worked on alternate tasks.

LESSON 11 Closure and Celebration *(1 class period)*

LESSON SEQUENCE AND DESCRIPTION	TEACHER COMMENTARY
Sharing of student projects and further exploration of games. Give students a "chance" to share their original games or discuss how probabilities factor into existing games. Then provide free time for students to play different games.	This was a great way to end the unit!

Teacher Reflection on the Unit

Because math is so skill-based, you can fall into the trap of grouping solely on readiness. At times, readiness grouping is the best choice; but many mathematical concepts can be taught effectively using student learning profile and interest as the basis for instruction and grouping. In this unit, the many possible methods for exploring probability invited alternate strategies for instruction and I mixed up my groupings to give students many ways to process and understand the unit's main ideas. The most effective lessons considered students' interests and varied learning profiles. It's not always easy to approach planning this way in math, but I owe it to my students to provide them with as many meaningful ways as possible to make of sense of what they are learning and help them see how what we study relates to their lives.

Laura C. Massey has a degree in gifted education and has taught elementary students in Georgia and North Carolina. She can be reached at MasseyLaura@aol.com.

SAMPLE 5.1—Unit Pre-Assessment

1. Tell whether each event is *certain, impossible, likely,* or *unlikely*:
   a. Spinning an even number on a spinner labeled *2, 4, 6,* and *8*.
   b. Pulling out a blue chip from a bag with nine blue chips and one red chip.
   c. Snow falling in Florida in July.
   d. Rolling a die without it landing on 6.
   e. Pulling out a consonant from a bag containing five tiles labeled *A, E, I, O,* and *U*.

2. What are the chances that a penny will land on heads?

3. How many outcomes exist when one die is rolled?

4. If you had three blue chips and one red chip in a bag, what is the probability that you will pull out a blue chip?

5. If there is a 1/6 chance that you will win the race, what is the probability that you will not win the race?

6. It is predicted that the Bears will win one out of four games. What is their percentage chance of winning the first game?

7. You are given the choice of a PB&J, grilled cheese, or a ham sandwich with either milk or orange juice. How many combinations are possible for your lunch?

8. Marshall has 15 cents. What are all of the different combinations of coins he could have?

9. If Marshall has only two coins and is willing to let you choose one from a bag, what are the chances that you will pull out a dime?

10. Write 1/4 as a decimal and as a percentage.

11. Write 40% as a decimal and as a fraction.

12. There are 10 students who ride the bus to school, 8 who ride in a car, and 5 who walk. Make a graph to represent these data.

SAMPLE 5.2—Mathematics Self-Assessment

Directions: Rate yourself along the scale for each of the following statements:

I enjoy math.

Never	Sometimes	Always

I am good at math.

Never	Sometimes	Always

I am a good problem solver.

Never	Sometimes	Always

I know a lot about probability and statistics.

Never	Sometimes	Always

I know a lot about fractions, decimals, and percentages.

Never	Sometimes	Always

I understand graphs.

Never	Sometimes	Always

I work well with others.

Never	Sometimes	Always

Finish each of the following statements:

My favorite part of math is . . .

My least favorite part of math is . . .

What I know about probability is . . .

What I want to know about probability is . . .

When we study probability, I hope we . . .

SAMPLE 5.3—Generalizations About Chance Homework Assignment

Directions: List at least three examples of real-life events that would fit under each unit generalization. Be prepared to share your examples with others in class.

Chance is the occurrence of an event with no apparent cause.

Chance is random.

We can determine the chance that an event will occur.

Patterns help us determine chances.

We can predict the occurrence of a single event by the number of possible outcomes.

SAMPLE 5.4—Creating a Character Worksheet

Follow the directions carefully. As you complete each step, think about how many options you used and how many outcomes you found.

Directions: Draw three heads, three bodies, and three sets of legs on each of the nine cards (one body part on each card). You will use the cards to create different characters. You may create any type of character you like (person, animal, fantastical creature).

After you complete your drawings, manipulate the cards to complete the following tasks. Record your findings in the chart.

1. Make as many different characters as you can using . . .
   a. Two heads, two bodies, and two sets of legs.
   b. One head, two bodies, and two sets of legs.
   c. Two heads, two bodies, and three sets of legs.
   d. Three heads, three bodies, and three sets of legs.
   e. One head, one body, and one set of legs.
   f. Three heads, two bodies, and three sets of legs.

# OF HEADS	# OF BODIES	# OF SETS OF LEGS	# OF CHARACTERS

2. Describe any patterns you see.

3. Think about all of the mathematical operations and see if you can discover the formula for finding all possible outcomes.

SAMPLE 5.5—Super Solver Problems

1. Given the letters *A, B, C, D,* and *E,* how many permutations that consist of only three letters can be created?

2. If eight people are competing in a race, how many different ways can medals be awarded for first, second, and third place?

3. A license plate can consist of three numbers and then three letters. How many possible license plate combinations exist?

4. There are six students in a group. How many different ways can these six students stand in a line?

5. Eight students in the class are running for the student council. Four of the students are girls and four are boys. Each class can elect two representatives—one girl and one boy. How many different possible combinations exist for the student council positions in this class?

6. You have seven picture frames, but only four will fit on the shelf. How many different ways can you arrange the picture frames on the shelf?

7. Your teacher wants you to help create a word scramble for the students. Scramble the letters in these words: *run, gallop, crawl,* and *skip.* How many possibilities are there for each of the words?

8. The school basketball team consists of eight players. Twenty people tried out for the team. How many different teams are possible?

9. You and five other people have entered a drawing for a free movie rental. Two names will be pulled. What are your chances of winning the free movie rental?

6

We Each Have
a Role to Play

*A Language Arts Unit Introducing
Literature Circles*

Unit Developer: Sandra Williams Page

Introduction

This three- to-four-week language arts unit uses various selections of fiction related to the concepts of **responsibility** and **choice** as a backdrop for introducing students to literature circles, a format for collaborative discussions developed by Harvey Daniels in his 1994 book *Literature Circles: Voice and Choice in the Student-Centered Classroom*. Literature circles include defined roles for participants to play as they work together to analyze and understand a text. Students usually meet in groups of six to eight, and participation is required of all students in each group. Because both student roles and the structure and pace of the discussion are defined, no one person or topic dominates the discussion, and all share responsibility for the discussion's flow and effectiveness. A key advantage of literature circles is that their small-group format can make participation in discussions feel "safer" to students who might otherwise be reluctant to speak in a group.

Establishing the literature circle routine takes time, and this unit is designed for the beginning of the school year. While focusing on characterization in stories, students learn about three literature circles roles (Discussion Director, Character Creator, and Literary Luminary) and then practice and apply these roles as they read fiction selected to resonate thematically with the requirements of literature circle participation (**responsibility** and **choice**). Class time is provided for reading and preparing for literature circle discussions. In addition, students have several opportunities to respond in writing to a variety of prompts. These prompts give students chances to connect with the material and skills presented during the unit and provide assessment information regarding student understanding.

Teacher Reflection on Designing the Unit

As elementary students become more fluent readers, it is appropriate to move beyond a focus on reading comprehension and to work to develop students' understanding of the elements of literature: setting, characterization, time and pacing, conflict, author's purpose, voice, and so on. I knew I wanted my students to begin to relate literature to their own lives so that they might be able to consider how a story can reveal things about themselves, their world, and their choices and create their own interpretations of what they read. I also knew that students seem to enjoy discussions of literature more if they can actively participate in them.

When I sat down to design this unit, then, my aim was to introduce students to the processes of literature circles—a format I knew I wanted to use throughout the year. The idea was to introduce a few key roles and then give students time to practice them with literature that focuses on some of the principles that underlie responsible group membership.

After I had determined what I wanted to teach, I turned to the challenge of differentiating the content to accommodate the varying readiness levels in my classroom. My solution was to create differentiated role descriptions that would challenge learners working at different levels of proficiency in reading and literary analysis. Once I had done this, it was simple to create tasks that were appropriate for all students, including those who struggle mightily, those who are very advanced, and those who are learning English.

Language Arts Standards Addressed
- Apply enabling strategies and skills to read and write.
- Apply strategies and skills to comprehend text that is read, heard, and viewed.
- Make inferences, draw conclusions, make generalizations, and provide support for ideas by referencing the text.
- Listen actively.
- Make connections with text through the use of oral language, written language, and media and technology.
- Apply strategies and skills to create oral, written, and visual texts.
- Use planning strategies to generate topics and organize ideas.

Unit Concepts and Generalizations
Responsibility, Choice
- Responsibility and choice are interrelated.
- We all have responsibilities.

- We are required to make choices all the time.
- Choices can have both good and bad consequences.
- Making thoughtful choices is part of being responsible.

Unit Objectives

As a result of this unit, the students will *know*

- Elements of characterization, including description, emotion, tone of voice, and actions.
- The tasks of specific literature circle roles.
- Criteria for asking and writing good questions.

As a result of this unit, the students will *understand that*

- People share responsibility for success when they work together.
- Passages from texts can reveal a character's personality.
- Accepting responsibility shows maturity.
- Making thoughtful choices is part of responsible behavior.
- Choices can have both good and bad consequences.

As a result of this unit, the students will *be able to*

- Plan and carry out personal responsibilities for group discussions.
- Ask thought-provoking questions.
- Listen actively.
- Draw conclusions.
- Make predictions based on textual clues.
- Analyze character actions and statements.
- Respond to literature through writing.
- Participate in student-led discussions.
- Relate literature to personal and community events.

Instructional Strategies Used

- Brainstorming
- Differentiated discussions
- Journal prompts based on student interest and readiness
- Mini-workshops
- Small-group discussions
- Tiered assessment
- Tiered assignments

Sample Supporting Materials Provided

Unit Overview

LESSON	WHOLE-CLASS COMPONENTS	DIFFERENTIATED COMPONENTS
LESSON 1 **Introduction to Literature Circles** *1 class period*	Overview of literature circles *10 minutes* Introduction of the Discussion Director role *10 minutes* Read-aloud and role modeling *20 minutes* Small-group discussions using prepared questions *15 minutes* Student evaluations of group discussions *5 minutes*	Journal responses based on student choice *10 minutes*
LESSON 2 **Asking Thoughtful Questions** *3 class periods*	Review and introduction of "thoughtful questions" *20 minutes* Brainstorming/refining thoughtful questions based on short text *20 minutes* Small-group discussions using class-generated questions *25 minutes*	

LESSON	WHOLE-CLASS COMPONENTS	DIFFERENTIATED COMPONENTS
	Journal prompt and whole-group discussion *15 minutes*	Individual/small-group discussions for students who struggle with writing
	Introduction of the Character Creator role *10 minutes*	
		Differentiated tasks based on readiness *40 minutes*
	Small-group discussions with student-generated questions *35–45 minutes*	Roles within groups differentiated based on readiness
	Evaluation of group work *10 minutes*	
LESSON 3 **Finding Big Ideas** *1–2 class periods*	Class discussion of **responsibility** *10 minutes*	
	Read-aloud modeling reading comprehension strategies *15 minutes*	
	Partner-work based on reading *20 minutes*	
	Introduction of the Literary Luminary role *5 minutes*	
		Journal prompts based on student interest *15–30 minutes*
	Sharing of journal responses *10 minutes*	

LESSON	WHOLE-CLASS COMPONENTS	DIFFERENTIATED COMPONENTS
LESSON 4 **Putting It All Together** *partial class periods over a 2-week time frame*		Book selection and literature circle group assignments, based on readiness and student choice *30 minutes*
	Individual work to read and prepare for the first round of literature circle discussions *2–3 class periods, 30 minutes per session*	Mini-workshops to address literature circle role responsibilities, reading comprehension strategies, and time management *as needed over the same 2–3 class sessions*
		Literature circle discussions differentiated by reading skills, roles and levels of tasks, and student choice of books *35–45 minutes*
	Evaluation of literature circle discussions *10 minutes*	
	Debriefing on the literature circle process *10 minutes*	
LESSON 5 **Adjusting and Tweaking** *partial class periods over a 2-week time frame*	Development of literature circle ground rules *15 minutes*	
	Individual work to read and prepare for the second round of literature circle discussions *2–3 class periods, 30 minutes per session*	Mini-workshops to address literature circle role responsibilities, reading comprehension strategies, and time management *as needed over the same 2–3 class periods*
		Literature circle discussions differentiated by reading skills, roles and levels of tasks, and student choice of books *35–45 minutes*
		Journal prompt based on student choice *15 minutes*

LESSON	WHOLE-CLASS COMPONENTS	DIFFERENTIATED COMPONENTS
	"A Few Thoughtful Questions" activity *15 minutes*	
	Individual work to read and prepare for the third round of literature circle discussions *2–3 class periods, 30 minutes per session*	
		Literature circle discussions differentiated by reading skills, roles and levels of tasks, and student choice of books *35–45 minutes*
LESSON 6 **Unit Assessment** *1 class period*		Tiered assessment based on readiness *35–45 minutes*

Literature Circles

My interpretation and application of literature circles focuses on students posing and responding to questions in every role. This prevents a "reporting" level of participation and instead offers students chances to ask and answer more interpretative questions. I introduce my students to most of the literature circle roles and processes at the start of the school year, beginning with the three that this unit addresses: Discussion Director, Character Creator, and Literary Luminary. As we progress through the first quarter of the year, I introduce additional literature circle roles, among them the Illustrator, the Connector, the Vocabulary/Linguist, and the Time/Travel Tracer. You can find more information about these roles in Daniels's *Literature Circles* (1994) and in Day, Spiegel, McLellan, and Brown's *Moving Forward with Literature Circles* (2002).

After the first month of school, I devote one day each week to literature circle discussions. The discussions usually take about 35–45 minutes, with additional time for reflection and responsive writing. Students also need time to prepare for their literature circle discussions. In this unit—again, slated for the beginning of the school year—I provide class time for this purpose and for them to actually read the literature selections. As the year progresses, however, much of this work becomes homework.

Teacher Reflection on Using Literature Circles

I use literature circles in my classroom because my students enjoy and benefit from the responsibility that they require. As a teacher, I facilitate the discussion groups, but they're really "run" by the students. In addition, I like the fact that the various roles in literature circles are flexible enough to allow for differences in my students' reading and thinking readiness. Using literature circles makes it quite easy to involve a full range of students in challenging and meaningful ways. Once my students have the skills they need to participate in literature circles, I can shift my focus to creating the differentiated roles and tasks that are necessary to meet their varying needs as we explore literature.

I've also found that literature circles provide an ideal vehicle for helping students learn to respect and appreciate the varied contributions of everyone in the class. To me, literature circles are also the best setting for exploring literature and for building social/community skills such as discussion, cooperation, delegation of responsibility, and respecting the ideas of others.

Unit Description and Teacher Commentary

LESSON 1	Introduction to Literature Circles	(1 class period)
LESSON SEQUENCE AND DESCRIPTION		TEACHER COMMENTARY
Overview of literature circles. Begin the lesson by explaining to the students that in this classroom, much of their work with literature will be done through small-group discussions called *literature circles*. Tell them that all group members will participate in discussions and that, usually, each person in the group will have a specific role to play. Other big ideas about literature circles to share with the students include the following: • Students have choices about what to read. • Different literature circles will read different books. • Literature circles will be formed based on book choice. • Questions will help focus the discussions to explore the students' ideas and their interpretations of their reading. • Evaluation of students will focus on group participation and collaboration as well as on content and skills knowledge. Explain these ideas so that the class understands them before you move on to describing roles. Involve the students in figuring out what the ideas will mean for them personally.		My students like to know where they're headed in my class, and I find that they are much more likely to "accompany me on the journey" if they have some idea about my plans. For this reason, I began this unit by sharing the basic principles that would guide our literature circle work and discussing how our class would adhere to those principles.

LESSON SEQUENCE AND DESCRIPTION	TEACHER COMMENTARY
Introduction of the Discussion Director role. Explain to students that the Discussion Director develops a list of questions than can help his or her group talk about big ideas in a reading and share their reactions to the reading. Sometimes the Discussion Director poses some specific topics or questions in advance so that students can think about them before the group discussion.	In addition to sharing this information verbally, I posted the role description in the classroom so that we could all "stay on the same page" about what this role requires.
Show the **Differentiated Discussion Director Role Description Cards** (see Sample 6.1, page 181) and explain that you have prepared two different formats of the description to address varying student needs. Share both description formats with the class, but only distribute the description cards to the students as needed. This cuts down on confusion about who should do what in which role.	Providing differentiated role descriptions challenges more sophisticated thinkers to pose more complex questions. It also allows me to provide question stems for readers who might otherwise create questions that only elicit knowledge-level or yes/no responses. Color-coding readiness levels allows for easy identification and communication. In the samples at the end of this unit, the "Blue" version of the role description cards is designed for lower-readiness students. The "Green" version is for higher-readiness students. For students with severe difficulty in reading, writing, and analyzing ideas, I provided a list of questions from which they, as Discussion Directors, could select.
Read-aloud and role modeling. Read aloud a short story or portion of a chapter from a novel that includes strong character development (for example, "I Learn Firefighting" from Ann Cameron's *More Stories Julian Tells*).	I like to use picture books and allow students to sit on the floor near me as I read. However, I do try to limit read-alouds to 15–20 minutes so that we can move on to working with the text.
Model what the Discussion Director does by sharing three or four questions you have created about the story/text on an overhead or poster. Focus on questions that draw on personal experiences, expository references, and analysis of characters' behaviors and thinking. Here is a sample set: • Julian and Huey are brothers. Can you think of ways they are like brothers you know?	This modeling allowed me to show my students exactly what I expected them to do as Discussion Director. I also posted the questions so that the students could refer back to them as needed.

LESSON SEQUENCE AND DESCRIPTION	TEACHER COMMENTARY
• Huey was reluctant to jump from the swing. What kinds of things did he do and say to delay the jump? • Julian thought his father was going to punish him when Huey got hurt. Did you think so too? Explain your thoughts. • Julian says, "I would like to be the person who sees the little spark that starts trouble and puts it out, like a forest fire, right at the beginning." What sparks did Julian *not see* that got his brother Huey and him into trouble?	My goal was to involve the students in talking about the kinds of questions I created and help them understand why I didn't create questions that allowed for simple answers. As I read these questions aloud, I paused to explain new vocabulary as needed.
Small-group discussions using prepared questions. Divide the class into random groups of four to six students. Explain that each group will have 10 minutes to discuss the text using one of the questions provided.	At this stage, while students were first learning about literature circles and how they work, I divided the class into random, heterogeneous groups. Literature circle groups can also be grouped based on readiness levels, interest, leadership abilities, learning profile, and gender.
Appoint one student in each group to be the Discussion Director. This student will begin the discussion by choosing and posing a question. This student will also need to ensure that every member of the group has a chance to speak. The group does not have to discuss every question.	For this first discussion, I picked Discussion Directors who could get the discussions started quickly but not dominate them.
Tell the groups that they will be evaluated based on the following criteria: • Everyone must speak about the question. • Everyone must listen respectfully. • Voices must be kept at a moderate level.	Before the discussions began, I reviewed the requirements for listening and speaking. Sometimes students need to be reminded about what it means to listen respectfully.
As the groups work, move around the room making notes about participation levels and providing assistance as needed.	My notes informed later grouping decisions and allowed me to provide the rest of the class with examples of students who helped peers with responses, listened well, and participated effectively in the discussions.
Student evaluations of group discussions. After 10 minutes, stop the group discussions and tell the class that literature circles will take place again the next day. Then give the groups several minutes to debrief about their discussions: Did everyone speak up and listen? Were voices kept to an acceptable level? How might the group improve its discussion?	Reflection time helps students understand the discussion requirements more fully and improves the quality of discussions. I make it part of every literature circle routine, even when the students seem adept at group discussions.

LESSON SEQUENCE AND DESCRIPTION	TEACHER COMMENTARY
Journal responses based on student choice. As a closure activity, ask the students to respond individually in writing to their choice of the prepared questions. The sample set, again: • Julian and Huey are brothers. Can you think of ways they are like brothers you know? • Huey was reluctant to jump from the swing. What kinds of things did he do and say to delay the jump? • Julian thought his father was going to punish him when Huey got hurt. Did you think so too? Explain your thoughts. • Julian says, "I would like to be the person who sees the little spark that starts trouble and puts it out, like a forest fire, right at the beginning." What sparks did Julian *not see* that got his brother Huey and him into trouble? As students write, work individually with those who need support for writing or need coaching to push their thinking or writing further.	I included this journal activity so that students could work with a question that they didn't have a chance to discuss in their groups. (However, if they chose to respond to the same question they focused on in their small groups, that was okay, too.) I was also seeking some assessment data about students' ability to respond to their reading. Because I created a range of questions, students had some choice about how they would respond to the text. Often my struggling learners prefer to respond to texts based on personal experiences. The first question invites just that. During "coaching time," I make it a point to work with a wide range of students representing all readiness levels.

LESSON 2 — Asking Thoughtful Questions *(3 class periods)*

LESSON SEQUENCE AND DESCRIPTION	TEACHER COMMENTARY
Review and introduction of "thoughtful questions." Begin with a quick review of the previous lesson's discussion of literature circles and the role of the Discussion Director. Then tell the students that today they will work on creating questions, just as they'll do when they are the Discussion Director. Ask: What makes a thoughtful question? Allow students to share their ideas. Then post the following list of criteria and relate students' contributions to what's on the list.	Asking thoughtful questions is a skill that students need to work on throughout the year and in every subject area. Each of the literature circle roles introduced in this unit involves asking thoughtful questions. Many elementary-age students know how to ask "closed" questions—Who, What, Where, Why, and How—with one right answer that can be found in the text.

LESSON SEQUENCE AND DESCRIPTION	TEACHER COMMENTARY
Thoughtful Questions . . . 1. Require explanation, not just "yes" or "no." 2. Cause us to think about the story, poem, article, or book. 3. Ask us to connect the reading to our own lives, ideas, and experiences. 4. Use strong verbs. 5. May refer to a specific action, character, or event in the reading. 6. Cause us to use our best thinking. Ask students to look back at the previous day's questions. Do they fit these criteria? How? To support the students' ongoing work with thoughtful questions, use this criteria list ("Six Criteria for Thoughtful Questions") as the cornerstone of a "question wall" on which you and the students continue to post examples of thoughtful questions and useful question stems.	In *Improving Comprehension with Think-Aloud Strategies* (2001), Jeff Wilhelm suggests that students comprehend better when they learn to generate and respond to a wide variety of questions. He lists four types, which I used to inform my thoughtful question criteria: • *Right There Questions:* The reader can find factual answers in the text. • *Think and Search Questions:* The reader needs to look for details and examples to arrive at an answer or inference. • *Author and Me Questions:* Answering requires the reader to think about what he or she already knows, what the author tells in the text, and how that fits together with the reader's thoughts and experiences. • *On Your Own Questions:* These questions arise from the story, but the answers come from the reader's own thoughts, not from the story.
Brainstorming/refining thoughtful questions based on short text. Explain to the students that in the coming weeks, they will be reading several books that all have to do with **responsibility** and **choice**. Read aloud (while the students read along silently) a typed page from one of the following novels: • *Hard Drive to Short* by Matt Christopher • *Lyddie* by Katherine Paterson • *Superfudge* by Judy Blume • *Maniac Magee* by Jerry Spinelli • *Let the Circle Be Unbroken* by Mildred Taylor	I kicked off the activity by calling attention to our unit concepts. Excerpts are a fine way to "sell" a book. I knew that I wanted students to read a book of their choosing later in the unit (see Lesson 4); this "preview" exposure was a way to help them make a more informed selection.

LESSON SEQUENCE AND DESCRIPTION	TEACHER COMMENTARY
	The day before this class, I gave ESL students a paper or audiotaped copy of the page I planned to read aloud so that they could prepare. Ensuring that ESL students can participate fully in literature circles requires coordination with the ESL specialist and the students' parents.
Lead a whole-group brainstorming session where students generate a class list of thoughtful questions related to the text. Remind them to think about the "Six Criteria for Thoughtful Questions" and **responsibility** and **choice.** Write the students' ideas on an overhead for all to see. Aim for about 15–20 questions.	When students asked questions that did not fit the criteria for thoughtful questions, I coached them to revise. For example, "That sounds like a "yes/no" question. How can we change it to make sure that it requires us to explain our thinking?"
After a few minutes, ask them to think about which questions would lead to the best discussions during literature circles. Narrow the list to three or four questions.	After we had discussed the options, I let the students vote for their favorite.
Small-group discussions using class-generated questions. Ask the students to return to their (heterogenous) literature circle groups from the previous lesson. Assign new Discussion Directors and distribute the appropriate differentiated role description cards. Remind everyone of the criteria for group discussions: 1. Everyone must speak about the question. 2. Everyone must listen respectfully. 3. Voices must be kept at a moderate level.	I posted the criteria for group discussions so that students could refer to them regularly.
Allow 20–30 minutes for the literature circles to meet to discuss the reading and the three or four questions the class has chosen. Remind students that the Discussion Director's role is to help the group stay focused and move through the questions. Move among the groups, making notes about group processes and individual participation and engagement.	
Journal prompt and whole-group discussion. Pose the following question and ask students to respond in writing: Which question caused you to think and learn the best? Why? When students have finished with their writing, ask them to share their ideas in the whole group.	My intent here was to have the students reflect on whether the questions they had generated brought about good discussions.

LESSON SEQUENCE AND DESCRIPTION	TEACHER COMMENTARY
	Because the goal of this assignment was reflection, I met (either one on one or in small groups) with students who struggled to express themselves in writing and we talked about this prompt.
Introduction of the Character Creator role. Tell students that within literature circles, the Character Creator is responsible for identifying and analyzing a major character in the text. Show the **Differentiated Character Creator Role Description Cards** (see Sample 6.2, page 182) and explain that the Character Creator serves as the expert on the character's thoughts, feelings, actions, perceptions, values, dreams, and motivations. The Character Creator makes statements about the character's behavior, words, and feelings and asks questions to help the group think about the character.	Again, in addition to reading the role descriptions to the class, I posted them for all to see.
Differentiated tasks based on readiness. Pass out a passage (three to six pages in length, from one of the novels mentioned previously) that includes information about a main character. Tell students that this passage will be the text for the next literature circle.	For struggling students, I arranged help with reading or listening to the text. To make sure all my students can access content, I often audiotape myself reading text passages. If they wish, students can read along while they listen to these tapes.
To help students prepare for the next literature circles, assign them to one of three tasks based on readiness level.	All three of these tasks address the unit concept of **responsibility.** One of my goals here was to find out what students already understood about this key concept. I used what I learned to inform role assignments for the next literature circle.
Task 1 (Struggling Students) 1. Read or listen to the passage. 2. Select one of the questions on the cards that you think would be a good discussion starter. 3. Work with a partner to give a thoughtful answer to the question you picked.	This task works well for students who have a lot of difficulty with reading and reasoning. I developed question choices appropriate for these students and then allowed them to work with partners to encourage greater participation and mutual support. Later, I asked these students to add their own questions to my list of options.

LESSON SEQUENCE AND DESCRIPTION	TEACHER COMMENTARY
Task 2 (On-Target Students) 1. Read the passage. 2. You have two choices here. Choice 1 is to write four or more questions that would be good discussion starters. Be sure to pose at least one question that has to do with **responsibility.** Choice 2 is to write four or more questions that get us to think about the actions, feelings, or thoughts of a main character in the story. Be sure to pose at least one question that has to do with **responsibility.** For example: • How does the character feel about certain people? • This character reacted to something that happened or was said (you should give a particular example of this from the story). What did the character do? How is that similar to what someone you know has done? • Which character would be a friend of yours? Why? 3. Use the "Six Criteria for Thoughtful Questions" to improve your questions.	Task 2 is more open-ended than Task 1. It asks students to create their own questions based on their reading and then choose how to focus those questions.
Task 3 (Advanced Students) 1. Read the passage. 2. Write four or more statements about an important character. Then, pose questions that ask about that character's words or behaviors and that would lead to a good discussion. Relate at least one question to the topic of **responsibility.** For example: • The character (give the name) acted foolishly when he _____. Do you think he should be punished for his behavior? • One example of how this character did or did not show responsibility was when he/she _____ . What were the consequences of this? • Often, main characters have counterparts in the story who cause them to have to confront a weakness or problem in themselves. Can you find an example of that counterpart in this passage? 3. Use the "Six Criteria for Thoughtful Questions" to improve your questions.	Task 3 is similar to but more complex than Task 2 because it asks the students to make a statement based on the text and then create a discussion question. Notice that even my higher-ability students got example questions. (I removed this scaffolding as they gained familiarity with the format.)

LESSON SEQUENCE AND DESCRIPTION	TEACHER COMMENTARY
Have all students reread the passage (possibly for homework) so that they will be prepared for their next literature circles. Be sure that students who need support in reading the passage have additional reading or listening time in class, a tape to take home, or an adult or peer who will help with the reading.	
Small-group discussions with student-generated questions. Ask students to reassemble in the literature circles they've been working in and then pass out the appropriately colored Discussion Director and Character Creator cards (see Sample 6.1 and Sample 6.2) to selected students in each group. The groups will use the questions they developed for their differentiated tasks as the basis for the discussion of the passage. (Because the groups are heterogeneous, there should be an even distribution of questions from Tasks 1, 2, and 3.) Remind students of the criteria for group discussions and tell them that you will give them a five-minute warning before the discussion is to end.	Again, I based role assignments on student readiness with regard to the ability to read and analyze text and think complexly. I also made sure to assign roles to students who had not yet played a specific role. I have found that my reluctant speakers generally benefit from the structure of having a role and that students who tend to be off-task pay better attention when they have the added responsibility a role entails.
Evaluation of group work. Conclude the lesson by reassembling as a class and using a "plus/delta" ($+/\Delta$) format to evaluate the day's literature circle. Leading questions to use include "What went particularly well today in the discussions? Why?" and "What might make the literature circle discussions even better?" Use an overhead or chart paper divided into two columns to better show the students' ideas, writing positive comments under the plus sign and changes that would make the discussions better under the delta sign. Keep the students' ideas posted for future literature circles.	"Plus/delta" is a great evaluation tool that is often used with adults. It can be very useful with students, too!

LESSON 3   **Finding Big Ideas**   *(1–2 class periods)*

LESSON SEQUENCE AND DESCRIPTION	TEACHER COMMENTARY
Class discussion of responsibility. Begin this lesson by asking students what **responsibilities** they have at home. For example, do they help make or clean up after dinner?	This quick discussion gave students a chance to relate personally to one of our big ideas for this unit before we looked at it in literature.

LESSON SEQUENCE AND DESCRIPTION	TEACHER COMMENTARY
Read-aloud modeling reading comprehension strategies. Explain to students that for this lesson, you will be reading the first two chapters of a book (Matt Christopher's *Hard Drive to Short*) out loud while they read along silently. Give them a brief overview of what you'll be reading and tell them that you want them to listen for anything having to do with **responsibility** or **choice**. Stress that this is the purpose for the reading.	I've found that my students pick up on reading comprehension strategies and use them more readily if I go over the strategies and model them in class.
Post the following strategies in the classroom so that you and the students can refer to them throughout the read-aloud: • Set a purpose for the reading. • Make predictions. • Find personal connections to my experiences. • Visualize what is happening. • Check that I understand what I've read. • Try some different ways to figure out something if I am confused or do not understand. As you read, stop at various points and ask students to make predictions about what is going to happen. Also, as you come to places where you want the students to visualize (see in their minds) what is happening, stop and give them a chance to do so. Finally, be sure to monitor their understanding of terms and sayings such as "let the ball hit the wood," "the ball dribbled toward the pitcher," and "beelined for first."	These strategies are addressed in depth in Jeff Wilhelm's *Improving Comprehension with Think-Aloud Strategies* (2001).
Partner-work based on reading. After reading the selection aloud and discussing the comprehension strategies used, allow the students to work in self-selected pairs to find a passage that shows Sandy making a **choice** and a passage in which he shows **responsibility.** Provide time for the pairs to share their ideas with the whole class. Ask: What might be the consequences of these choices? What would happen if Sandy did not show responsibility?	Because I often assign students to groups, I like to find opportunities for them to choose someone to work with. This was an easy place to do that. Here, I wanted the students to start thinking about and discussing the concepts of **responsibility** and **choice.**
Introduction of the Literary Luminary role. Tell students that the third role in literacy circles is that of the Literary Luminary. Show the **Differentiated Literary Luminary Role Description Cards** (see Sample 6.3, page 183) and explain that the person in this role focuses attention on particularly important or relevant passages in the text or reading that show changes in the story or in a particular character.	Again, I also posted the role descriptions in the classroom.

LESSON SEQUENCE AND DESCRIPTION	TEACHER COMMENTARY
The Literary Luminary poses questions that invite the rest of the circle to consider specific passages and these passages' impact on the story or article.	
Journal prompts based on student interest. Give the students about 15 minutes to select and write in response to one of the following prompts: *Prompt 1* Imagine that Sandy did not go home on time. Predict what would happen next. *Prompt 2* What responsibilities will you have as you grow older? What will your responsibilities be when you are 12? Seventeen? A parent? *Prompt 3* When have you had to make a difficult choice, like Sandy did in leaving the baseball game? How did you feel? *Prompt 4* Sandy had responsibilities to his baseball team and to his family. Which responsibility should be more important? Defend why he should make the choice to go home or to stay and finish the game.	Although all four prompts require students to think about either **responsibility** or **choice,** the first and last prompts invite some high-level, skill-oriented thinking (predict, advocate, defend) while the second and third prompts ask for more personal responses. It's fine to privately encourage students who have great difficulty with lengthy writing to list their ideas or sketch and label their responses.
Sharing of journal responses. Provide time for students to share and discuss ideas from their writing. Either elicit responses from the class as a whole or set up groups of three or four students so that more students are actively engaging in the sharing.	The purpose of this discussion was for the students to hear ideas that might be different from their own.

LESSON 4	**Putting It All Together**	*(partial class periods over a 2-week time frame)*

LESSON SEQUENCE AND DESCRIPTION	TEACHER COMMENTARY
Note: In this lesson and the next, both of which are spread out over several class sessions, students will read a book of their choosing and participate in three rounds of literature circles. In preparation, gather a selection of books that deal with the unit concepts of **responsibility** and **choice** and that represent a variety of readiness levels and interests. Next, divide each of the books into three logical sections.	

LESSON SEQUENCE AND DESCRIPTION	TEACHER COMMENTARY
Book selection and literature circle group assignments, based on readiness and student choice. Show students the books that they are to choose from. Here are some options:	I helped students to make wise choices of books that were suitable to their readiness levels. For example, among the titles listed here, *Amos and Boris* and *More Stories Julian Tells* are appropriate books for struggling readers. *Hard Drive to Short* and *Altogether, One at a Time* are slightly more difficult in terms of reading level. *Maniac Magee* and *Superfudge* are another step up, and *Lyddie* and *Let the Circle Be Unbroken* are the most challenging of the group. If a student was interested in reading a book slightly above or below his or her reading level, I allowed that student to do so.

- *Amos and Boris* by William Steig
- *More Stories Julian Tells* by Ann Cameron
- *Hard Drive to Short* by Matt Christopher
- *Altogether, One at a Time* by E. L. Konigsburg
- *Maniac Magee* by Jerry Spinelli
- *Superfudge* by Judy Blume
- *Lyddie* by Katherine Paterson
- *Let the Circle Be Unbroken* by Mildred Taylor

Provide brief descriptions of the books and remind students of the excerpts you presented earlier in the unit. Help students make selections as necessary to ensure that they are appropriately challenged (their selections are not too easy, not too hard).	
Hand out index cards and ask students to write their names on the cards and then rank their first through third choices.	While I want students to have a say about what they read, I do not want them to choose based on what their friends are choosing. Here, I used index cards to keep the choices confidential.
Between class sessions, review students' preference lists and create groups of at least three students (ideally, six to eight students) who will read the same book. If more than eight students want to read the same book, create more than one literature circle for that book.	My goal was to group students with similar readiness levels while accommodating student preference in titles and achieving a balance of interests and genders.
Individual work to read and prepare for the first round of literature circle discussions. Set a date for the first literature circles that gives the students in all groups a chance to complete the first third of their book and prepare to discuss it.	
For the first literature circle, ask for volunteers to play the roles of Discussion Director, Character Creator, and Literary Luminary. Inform the students that they will all practice a role while reading this round of books.	I gave the students who were taking on roles the appropriate role description cards, differentiated by readiness levels. This ensured that strong readers and thinkers who were reading a slightly easier book still had a more sophisticated role to play. Likewise, students struggling with reading and/or responding to literature received role description cards that matched their readiness levels.

LESSON SEQUENCE AND DESCRIPTION	TEACHER COMMENTARY
Mini-workshops to address literature circle role responsibilities, reading comprehension strategies, and time management. As students read in class and prepare for their discussions, provide assistance as needed. It can be helpful to ask the students playing particular roles to meet in small groups to give each other feedback and assistance as they prepare for their literature circles. Possible topics for role-related mini-workshops include identifying keywords, creating organizers, and selecting and developing statements about important ideas. Remember that "role-playing" students who have severe difficulty reading, writing, and analyzing may need additional practice asking questions and leading discussions. To help struggling readers finish the first third of their books by the first literature circle date, consider supplying audiotape versions, enlisting the assistance of resource teachers and parents, and using small-group guided reading. In addition, allowing students to read alone or with partners at least some of the time is a great learning profile differentiation that can be quite helpful to some learners.	I used mini-workshops so that I could target the specific needs of individual students or small groups of students. I find that focused, need-based instruction highlighting particular skills is often a more efficient and effective use of time than whole-group instruction.
Literature circle discussions differentiated by reading skills, roles and levels of tasks, and student choice of books. On the set date, place the students in their literature circle groups to discuss the first third of their novels. Quickly review the criteria for discussion participation and pass out the appropriate copies of the role description cards. Allow 35–45 minutes for the literature circles, and at the end of this time frame, be sure give the groups 10- and 5-minute warnings so that they can make sure that everyone has a chance to contribute and participate. Discussion Directors should start the discussion, though all students are responsible for asking questions and providing responses. As students discuss, move among them, stopping to listen to and, if needed, spur discussions. Good lead-ins to get the students thinking on their own include questions that begin with "I wonder whether . . ." and "Have you thought about . . ."	Again, I based these groups primarily on student choice and readiness levels, but I also considered interests, gender, and personalities as I finalized group membership. I monitored these discussions carefully—first, to ensure that the groups were discussing ideas rather than just retelling the stories and second, to take notes on individuals' participation levels and who seemed to be struggling with reading level or content. The notes guided my grouping decisions for future literature circles.

LESSON SEQUENCE AND DESCRIPTION	TEACHER COMMENTARY
Evaluation of literature circle discussions. After the first round of literature circles, ask each group to use the plus/delta format to evaluate their discussions. In addition, pass out index cards and ask students to complete individual self-evaluations. They should name two things they personally did well during the discussion and two ways that they can improve during the next discussions.	I find that both group evaluations and self-evaluations lead to real growth in my students' abilities to cooperate, listen to one another, and think about literature. While they certainly need (and receive) evaluations from me, they need chances to reflect personally about their own performance.
Debriefing on the literature circle process. Before moving on to the next round of literature circles, lead a whole-class discussion about the literature circle process. Questions to explore include what is working and what could be improved, what students like and do not like about this process, and how it has changed the way they look at books.	A whole-class debriefing is a useful tool for further assessment. Here, it also provided time for the class to consider the process as a whole and for groups to hear what others think about the process and how they are applying it. In that sense, it was an opportunity for students to learn from one another.

LESSON 5   **Adjusting and Tweaking**   *(partial class periods over a 2-week time frame)*

LESSON SEQUENCE AND DESCRIPTION	TEACHER COMMENTARY
Development of literature circle ground rules. Based on the group and self-evaluations students submit and the whole-group discussion that concluded Lesson 4, work with the class to brainstorm and finalize a set of formal ground rules for literature circles. Here are some examples: • Everyone participates. • No off-task conversations or other activities during literature circles. • If you disagree, speak kindly and respectfully and give specific details to support your opinion. • Build on what someone else has just said, using phrases such as "Just like John, I thought . . . " • Take time to listen. • Ask questions directed to people who have not had a chance to speak up ("What do you think?"). • Be prepared. • Move on to another question after everyone has spoken once.	I posted the ground rules in the classroom so that groups could refer to them as needed.

LESSON SEQUENCE AND DESCRIPTION	TEACHER COMMENTARY
Individual work to read and prepare for the second round of literature circle discussions. Announce the date for the second literature circles and give students class time to read the next third of their books and prepare for the discussion. Within each of the groups, reassign the roles of Discussion Director, Character Creator, and Literary Luminary, choosing students who have not yet played a role.	As my students' familiarity with literature circles grows, I often ask them to play particular roles for the duration of a book or novel. However, in this unit—their first exposure to the process—I thought it was important for all students to get to practice at least one role.
Mini-workshops to address literature circle role responsibilities, reading comprehension strategies, and time management. While students are reading their novels, conduct these small-group sessions for students needing support.	Again, these mini-workshops helped me to address the specific needs of particular students.
Literature circle discussions differentiated by reading skills, roles and levels of tasks, and student choice of books. Students will follow the same procedures used during the previous literature circles. As before, monitor the discussions closely and pose questions as needed. Make sure to remind the students playing roles to pose questions that address **responsibility** and **choice.**	Another round of note-taking and informal assessment.
Journal prompt based on student choice. When the groups have completed the second-round discussions, tell students to select one of the following prompts to respond to individually in writing: *Prompt 1* Did the literature circle discussions cause you to change your opinion about this book or a character in the story? What do you think now? Why? *Prompt 2* Did anyone in your group share an idea that was a new thought for you? What was it? How has it affected your thinking? *Prompt 3* What questions do you have about the book that have not yet been answered? How might you go find answers to your questions?	These self-selected journal responses gave me another way to assess students' discussion participation and their ability to think about and understand their reading.

LESSON SEQUENCE AND DESCRIPTION	TEACHER COMMENTARY
"A Few Thoughtful Questions" activity. Reassemble the class as a large group and spend a few minutes discussing the second round of literature circles. Ask: What's working? What could still use some improvement?	I often find that my students think that asking a lot of questions is better than asking a few good ones. I used this exercise to get them thinking about whether or not more is truly better. My aim, of course, was for them to begin to create fewer— but more complex and thought-provoking—questions.
Next, prompt students to consider the *number* of questions they are discussing in their groups. Ask: Is it better to discuss many questions or just a few? Why do you say so?	
Show several photographs or pictures of artwork for about five seconds each. Then select one and display it while you share your observations about it (details, colors, subject matter, style). Ask: What is the difference between going through all these pictures quickly and spending time examining one closely? Which did you like better? Why? Which did you learn more from? Why? How might this relate to the questions we discuss in literature circles?	Here, I wanted to help students realize the importance of allowing everyone a chance to think about and respond to questions rather than rushing through.
At this point, you may wish to add another ground rule to your list: "Take time to think about questions; do not rush through them."	
Individual work to read and prepare for the third round of literature circle discussions. Continue using the literature circle process as students finish the final third of their novels.	I've found that my students really benefit from using the same process each time we do literature circles. The regularity means less guessing on their part, allowing them to really focus on asking and responding to the discussion questions. This is especially true for students who are struggling or those who benefit from structure in their routines.
Make sure to assign roles for the last literature circles so that all students have a chance to play at least one role. Remind them that they will have time over the course of the year to learn about and play other roles.	
✴**Literature circle discussions differentiated by reading skills, roles and levels of tasks, and student choice of books.** As you monitor the discussions and students' abilities to carry out their literature circle roles, look for indications that they have grown in their abilities to participate in discussions and understand literature: • Are they listening actively to others? • Are they asking thought-provoking questions? • Are they making logical predictions and drawing logical conclusions?	My assessment here focused on how students' skill levels were demonstrated in this third round of literature circles compared to their skill levels at the start of this unit.

LESSON 6	Unit Assessment	*(1 class period)*

LESSON SEQUENCE AND DESCRIPTION	TEACHER COMMENTARY
Tiered assessment based on readiness. Assign students to one of the following assessment tasks, differentiated to accommodate different readiness levels in regard to abstract and complex thinking.	This formal tiered assessment requires students to synthesize their thinking about **responsibility** and **choice** in the books that they read.
Level 1 Task Choose two of our five unit generalizations. Provide support for each of them using several examples from the book you read. You must provide at least four examples for each generalization. Be sure to think about your literature circle discussions.	I designed this task—which is concrete, specific, and structured—for my less abstract and complex thinkers. I looked for responses that were thoughtful and accurate, based on the stories and books the students read.
Level 2 Task Our class learned to share responsibility for learning by participating in literature circles. How are the **choices** made during the literature circles and the **responsibilities** required during them related to the stories we heard or read during this unit? To remind you, we heard stories about Julian and his little brother, and Sandy and his sisters, and you read a book with your group. What do these characters and our class have in common? Give at least five specific examples.	This task asks more abstract and complex thinkers to transfer their understanding of our unit concepts to the processes used during literature circles. I looked for responses that were insightful and accurate, based on the stories and books the students read.
As necessary, allow students who need support with writing to work with a resource teacher, to dictate their responses, or to tape record their responses.	I also provided lists of key words and phrases and highlighted books to support these students' writing.

Teacher Reflection on the Unit

I've conducted this unit at the beginning of several school years now, and it really sets the pace for what's to come. It gives the students a solid foundation for their future work with literature, and it gives me more than ample information about where my students are with regard to reading and analyzing literature, participating in discussions, and taking on leadership within groups. I continue to use this insight into their "starting points" to make instructional decisions as the year progresses and as we participate in more literature circles. Finally, I've found that the criteria for thoughtful questions presented here is very useful in other settings and subjects—for example, when I ask students to develop questions for history projects and figure out what's important in our science topics.

Sandra Williams Page has taught in Georgia and North Carolina and is currently a gifted program coordinator in North Carolina. She is also a consultant for ASCD. She can be reached at spage@chccs.k12.nc.us.

SAMPLE 6.1—Differentiated Discussion Director Role Description Cards

Discussion Director   **BLUE**

Your job is to begin the discussion and help manage time during the literature circle. To do this, you will need to

- Have several questions written out before the literature circle begins. Be sure to include questions that have many right answers, not just one.

- Call on people to share their ideas or talk about the passage/book from their literature circle role.

- Help the discussion process go smoothly by reminding members of the ground rules as needed.

Discussion Director   **GREEN**

Your job is to maintain the flow of the discussion. To do this, you will need to

- Make a statement about passage/book your group read, and then choose four or more discussion questions from a list that you have created. Make sure that your questions meet the criteria for good questions.
- Ask questions and provide responses that address the concepts of the passage or book.
- Ensure participation by inviting others to respond.
- Complete all roles within the discussion time limits.
- Ask an evaluative, summarizing question to end the day's discussion. This final question can deal with the group's work, the group members' opinions of this author or genre, or personal connections to the passage/book.

SAMPLE 6.2—Differentiated Character Creator Role Description Cards

Character Creator   **BLUE**

Your job is to help the group better understand a main character. To do this, you will need to

- Make notes about the character's thoughts, values, relationships, actions, words, and feelings. You may use a graphic organizer to take notes while reading and share with the group.

- Prepare two or three questions that ask the group to describe in detail what they know about the character.

- Create a diagram or illustration that shows people, interests, and ideas of particular importance to the character.

Character Creator   **GREEN**

Your job is to help the group analyze the main character. To do this, you will need to

- State the significance of particular words, actions, beliefs, misunderstandings, and relationships to the character. Which of these are most important? Why? Why are particular events, behaviors, conversations, and other characters important to the character?

- Develop a thesis ("big idea") statement that relates this character to one of the concepts we have discussed. Prepare several questions to spur discussion about this thesis statement.

- Compare this character to others we have read about and discuss what they have in common.

SAMPLE 6.3—Differentiated Literary Luminary Role Description Cards

Literary Luminary   **BLUE**

Your job is to pick out two or three passages in the book or reading that show important feelings, events, thoughts, or moments. To share these with your group, you will need to:

- Read the passages aloud, ask someone else to read them, or have the group read them silently.

- Write a sentence or statement that summarizes why these passages are important.

- Prepare one or two questions to help the group think about and discuss the passages.

Literary Luminary   **GREEN**

Your job is to pick out two or three passages in the book or reading that are crucial to the group's understanding of a moment in the story or a character's motivations, thoughts, behaviors, or emotions. To help your group focus on the importance of these passages, you will need to

- Read the passages aloud. If the passage is a dialogue, you may want to read it with another group member as if it is dialogue in a play.

- Write a statement that relates this passage to one of our concepts.

- Prepare one or two questions that ask for others' ideas and opinions about the passages.

Glossary

Anchor activities—These are tasks students automatically move to when they complete assigned work. Teachers may provide a list of possible anchor options and should encourage students to suggest other ideas. Anchor activities must be important to essential student learning and never just time-fillers. In classes with flexible pacing, all students will need anchor options. Still, if a student is consistently finishing work early, it's likely that either the student is finding the work too easy or the student is working at a lesser level of craftsmanship.

Big idea—This term is sometimes used as a synonym for a **generalization.** It refers to the key understandings a student should derive from a lesson or unit.

Concept—A concept is the name assigned to a category of objects or ideas with common attributes. Concepts are abstract, broad, and universal. They help learners make sense of ideas and information because they help organize and distinguish entities. They help learners look at likenesses and categorize objects and ideas. Concepts are generally stated in one word (for example, *pattern, probability, habitat, poem, perspective, energy, fraction, number, justice*). Sometimes concepts require two or three words to communicate an idea (for example, *rights and responsibilities, balance of power, checks and balances, relative size, supply and demand, central tendency, point of view*).

Concept-based teaching—Concept-based teaching uses the essential concepts and key principles of a discipline as the primary way of organizing curriculum content. For example, a teacher might tell her students that history is the study of "CREEPS." The acronym stands for *C*ulture, *R*eligion, *E*conomics, *E*sthetics, *P*olitics, and *S*ocial issues. Students define each of the concepts in their own words, and these concept definitions give students a yearlong (and, in fact, lifelong) lens for viewing history. It also helps them make connections between their own lives, current events, and historical events. Principles that relate to each concept help students think more specifically about patterns in history. One key principle they might examine is, "People shape culture and culture shapes people." Students can see how this principle plays out in history and in their own lives.

Equalizer—The Equalizer is a visual guide to help teachers think about tiering content, tasks, and products (*see* **Tiering**). As the figure here illustrates, it suggests several continua along which teachers can adjust task or product difficulty. By matching task difficulty with learner readiness, a teacher can provide appropriate challenge for a given learner at a given time. For example, if students in a math class are working with measurement, their teacher might ask them to measure the surface area of a desk. If the teacher asks students having difficulty with measurement to measure the surface area of their bedroom floors as a homework assignment, that task, on the Equalizer, would be relatively "foundational"—that is, similar to the familiar, in-class task. If, on the other hand, the teacher finds that some students have a solid grasp of the in-class task, the teacher might assign homework asking them to develop a plan for measuring the surface area of a tree. That task is much more "transformational," or unfamiliar. In this way, both groups of students can continue to advance their ability to measure surface area, but at appropriately different degrees of difficulty.

The Equalizer: A Tool for Planning Differentiated Lessons

Exit card—An exit card is a quick and easy method of assessing student understanding of a particular idea, skill, or topic. The teacher teaches the skill or concept that is central to the lesson and gives students a chance to work with it and discuss it. Just a few minutes before the day's lesson ends, the teacher distributes index cards to all students. Then, the teacher poses a question that probes student understanding of the topic

(rather than information recall) and asks students to write their name and a response to the question on their index card. Students turn in the card as they leave the room (or someone may collect the cards). The teacher does not grade the exit cards, but rather sorts them in categories representative of student understanding. A teacher might elect to use only two categories (students who seem to grasp the idea and those who don't) or might elect to use as many as four or five categories (students who understand little, understand some, have a basic understanding, have only a few gaps, and have a solid grasp). In this way, the exit cards become a vehicle for planning subsequent lessons aimed at helping each student continue to grow in knowledge and skill from a current point of understanding. As an alternative, teachers sometimes use a "3–2–1 format" on exit cards. In this instance, students might be asked to write the three most important ideas in the lesson, two questions they still have about the lesson, and one way they can use what they learned. Either approach can be modified to match lesson goals and learner needs.

Flexible grouping—Flexible grouping is purposeful reordering of students into working groups to ensure that all students work with a wide variety of classmates and in a wide range of contexts during a relatively short span of classroom time. Flexible grouping enables students to work with peers of both similar and dissimilar readiness levels, interests, and learning profiles, and allows the teacher to "audition" each student in a variety of arrangements. At various points in a lesson, most students have a need to work with peers at similar levels of readiness on a given topic or skill. But they also benefit from heterogeneous groupings in which the teacher takes care to ensure that each student has a significant contribution to make to the work of the group. Likewise, although most students enjoy the chance to work with peers whose interests (or learning profiles) match their own, they may be challenged and enriched by blending their interests (or learning profiles) with students of differing talents and interests (or learning profiles) to accomplish a task that draws on multiple interests (or approaches to learning). Additionally, it's important for students to work as a whole class, individually, and in small groups—and when doing so, to learn to make good choices related to working relationships. A teacher who uses flexible grouping systematically groups and regroups students as a regular feature of instructional planning.

Gender-based differentiation—It is likely that there are predominantly male learning preferences and predominantly female learning preferences. On the other hand, it is clearly the case that not *all* members of the same gender learn in the same ways. The goal of gender-based differentiation, then, is to understand the range of learning preferences that may be influenced by gender and to develop learning options that span that range, allowing students of either gender to work in ways that are most effective for them. Among the continua of learning preferences that may be gender-influenced are abstract versus concrete, still versus moving, collaboration versus competition, inductive versus deductive, and silent versus talking. Although there is great variance within each gender, *in general*, females prefer the first approach in each pair, and males the second. However, it is important to remember that there is great variance within each gender. Gender-based differentiation is one facet of learning profile differentiation.

Generalization—A generalization is an essential understanding central to a topic or discipline. It's a statement of truth about a concept. Generalizations transfer across events, times, and cultures. Like the concepts they help explain, generalizations are broad and abstract. Unlike concepts, generalizations are written as complete sentences. An example of a generalization is "Parts of a system are interdependent." Ensuring that students consistently work with generalizations helps them to understand what the topic is really about. It also promotes retention of information and transfer across and within topics.

Intelligence preference—According to psychologists such as Howard Gardner and Robert Sternberg, human brains are "wired" differently in different individuals.

Although all normally functioning people use all parts of their brains, each of us is "wired" to be better in some areas than we are in others. Gardner suggests eight possible intelligences, which he calls *verbal/linguistic, logical/mathematical, bodily/kinesthetic, visual/spatial, musical/rhythmic, interpersonal, intrapersonal,* and *naturalist* (see Gardner, 1993, 1997). Sternberg suggests three intelligence preferences: *analytic* (schoolhouse intelligence), *creative* (imaginative intelligence), and *practical* (contextual, street-smart intelligence) (see Sternberg, 1988, 1997). Differentiation based on a student's intelligence preference generally suggests allowing the student to work in a preferred mode and helping the student to develop that capacity further. Sometimes teachers also ask students to extend their preferred modes of working, or they opt to use a student's preferred areas to support growth in less comfortable areas. Differentiation based on intelligence preference is one kind of learning profile differentiation.

Interest-based differentiation—As learners, we are motivated by things that interest us, and we tend to be more confident in our ability to succeed when we work with those things. Interest-based differentiation attempts to tap into the interests of a particular learner as a means of facilitating learning. Interest-based differentiation can build upon existing interests or extend interests. Further, interest-based differentiation can link student interests with required learning outcomes or can provide students the opportunity to extend their own talents and interests beyond the scope of required learning goals.

Interest centers—These are a particular kind of **learning center.** Rather than focusing on mastery of required knowledge, information, and skills (as learning centers do), interest centers allow students to explore ideas or topics of particular interest to them in greater depth and/or breadth than would be possible in the prescribed curriculum. Interest centers can focus on topics derived directly from a unit of study. They can also address topics outside the curriculum. Teachers can differentiate interest centers by encouraging students to participate in those centers that address their particular interests, talents, or questions.

I Spy—I Spy is a game that can be played with small or large groups of students. The game leader (the teacher or a student) finds an object in the room that has a specific set of characteristics, and the players try to guess what the object is. For example, the leader might say, "I spy a blue object that has two sets of parallel lines." Players look around the room and name objects that fit that description until they select the correct one. This game requires students to apply understanding of target vocabulary, make observations, and use clues to draw accurate conclusions.

Jigsaw—This cooperative strategy, developed by Elliot Aronson (see Aronson et al., 1978), allows students to become experts in a facet of a topic they're particularly interested in. Students first meet in small groups, sometimes called *home-base groups*. Here, they review the task they must complete and clarify goals for individuals and the group. They then divide into specialty groups, or *work groups*. Each specialty group is responsible for one facet of the overall task. Every member of the specialty group works to develop a full understanding of the assigned subtopic or subtask. After an appropriate time, students reassemble in their home-base groups. Each member of the group shares the information about his or her specialty. All group members are responsible for asking questions and learning about all facets of the topic. In effective Jigsaw arrangements, all students are both teachers and learners. Teachers may assign students to specialty groups based on assessed needs or interests, or students may select their own. Appropriately used, Jigsaw can address readiness, interest, and learning profile needs.

Learning centers—Learning centers are a collection of materials and activities designed to teach, reinforce, or extend students' knowledge, understanding, and skills. Learning centers are often associated with physical spaces in the classroom, as many teachers set up center materials and activities in a particular area of the classroom and ask students to move to that area when it is

time to work "at the center." However, learning centers can also be more portable—"housed" in boxes or folders students use at designated times, then stored again when not in use. Students typically keep records of the work they do while at a learning center in order to account for what they have accomplished during each center visit. Learning centers can be differentiated by having students visit only those centers suited to their needs (compared with having all students move to all centers), by specifying tasks and materials at a given center for particular students based on those students' learning needs, and/or by adjusting the time an individual student spends at a particular center.

Learning contracts—A learning contract is an agreement between a student and a teacher regarding a task or project that a student will work on independently and with some freedom. Learning contracts often provide some degree of choice regarding specific tasks to be completed and the order in which they will be completed. This element of choice can help teachers address differences in students' interests and learning profiles. Effective contracts focus on key understandings and skills that a student is to work with and provide information about the criteria for quality work. Learning contracts require teachers to match learning objectives with contract options so that students must practice and apply important skills.

Learning stations—Learning stations are areas or regions in a classroom to which students move on a specified timetable to complete particular tasks. Learning stations are similar to **learning centers** and **interest centers**, but are less fixed than those kinds of centers tend to be. Learning stations can be differentiated by having students visit only those stations suited to their needs (compared with having all students move to all stations) and/or by specifying tasks and materials at a given station for particular students based on their learning needs.

Learning style—Learning style is one facet of a student's learning profile and refers to personal and environmental factors that may affect learning. For example, some students need quiet when they work, while others prefer interaction or some noise. Some students work best while sitting up straight at a table or desk; others learn best in a more relaxed position. Differentiation based on a student's learning style is one facet of learning profile differentiation.

List–Group–Label—This is a type of concept development activity in which students begin by listing words or ideas related to a particular topic. Next, students group items in the list so that they are arranged by common features. Finally, students label the categories to designate the feature that unites the items in that category. For example, if young learners had a list of animals, they might ultimately decide to put dogs, cats, goldfish, and hamsters in one category; starfish, whales, dolphins, and eels in a second; and pigs, cows, horses, and sheep in a third. Their categories might be "pets," "animals that live in the ocean," and "farm animals."

Metacognition—This term refers to students' thinking about their own thinking. (For example, a teacher might ask students to explain how they solved a problem or to monitor their understanding of a particular concept so that they might ask for clarification.) It is likely that students are more effective learners when they are aware of both the kind of thinking a particular instance calls for and the thinking processes they use to make this decision. It is important for teachers to help students develop a "vocabulary of thinking" and to monitor their own thinking processes.

Mini-workshops—This is another name for small-group instruction. When a teacher senses that some learners need additional help with a topic, understanding, or skill, the teacher might conduct a small-group teaching session on that topic to help learners make necessary progress. The teacher may open the mini-workshop to all students interested in attending, invite specific students to attend, or do both. A student who is particularly strong with a topic or skill might conduct a mini-workshop for peers, as long as the student is also effective in working with

agemates and teaching what he or she knows. Mini-workshops can be particularly helpful in guiding students through complex product assignments in which some requirements are not familiar to all learners. They are also useful for helping groups of students at all skill levels know how to move to a next level of proficiency.

Process log—A process log is a mechanism for helping students keep track of their thinking as they work on a product or other complex task. The goal of a process log is not so much to record concrete details such as the names of books read or the length of time spent working on a task; its main purpose is to help students think reflectively about their work (*see* **Metacognition**). What are their goals for a work session? Why have they selected those goals? How do they know whether they are on the right track with their work? What are they doing to achieve work at the highest possible level? When they get stuck, what do they do? These sorts of prompts may guide students as they write in their process logs. Typically, teachers collect and review process logs at assigned checkpoints while work is in progress and again when students turn in a finished product. The process log allows insight into the process of working *and* the product of the work.

RAFT activities—RAFTs take their name from the first letter of four words: Role, Audience, Format, and Topic. In a RAFT, students play a specified role, for a particular audience, in a named format, regarding a topic that gets at the core of meaning for that topic. For example, during a study of punctuation, a student may take on the role of a semicolon, for an audience of 5th graders, in the format of a personal letter, and on the topic, "I wish you really understood where I belong." RAFTs allow differentiation by readiness, interest, and learning profile.

Readiness-based differentiation—Our best understanding of how people learn is that they begin with past knowledge, understanding, and skill and extend those to new levels of complexity or sophistication. Further, we learn best when the work we do is a little too hard for us. What that means is that we have a sense of both what the task calls for and the gaps in our capacity to do what it asks of us. When these gaps are not present (in other words, when we can do a task effortlessly), we do not learn because we do not stretch what we already know. Similarly, when the gaps are too great, we cannot span them and do not learn. Learning takes place when we have to stretch a manageable amount and do so. Readiness-based differentiation attempts to design student work at varied levels of challenge so that each student has to stretch a manageable amount and is supported in doing so.

Rubrics—Rubrics are tools that guide the evaluation of student work and clarify student understanding of expectations for quality work. Generally, rubrics specify several categories of significance in achieving quality (for example, quality of research, quality of expression, and work habits). In addition, a rubric describes how various levels of quality in each of the designated categories would look. The most effective rubrics help students explore *qualitative* differences in their work, rather than quantitative differences. For example, it is not necessarily an indication that a student has done better work if he or she used five resources rather than four. A more appropriate indication of quality is that the student synthesized understandings from several reliable resources.

Scaffolding—Scaffolding refers to any support system that enables students to succeed with tasks they find genuinely challenging. Goals of scaffolding include helping students be clear about the task's purpose and directions and helping students stay focused, meet the expectations for quality of work, find and use appropriate sources of information, and work effectively and efficiently. The many types of scaffolding include study guides, step-by-step directions, comprehension strategies, use of a tape recording or video to support reading or understanding, modeling, icons that help interpret print, guided lectures, and multimode teaching. When tasks are appropriately challenging (a little too difficult for the student attempting the task), all students need scaffolding in order to grow and succeed.

Simulations—Simulations are activities designed to allow students to work as experts (or real people in general) might work with contexts or problems that are more authentic than is often the case in school. For example, students might simulate scientists trying to clean up a polluted area of a nearby estuary, or a family going west during the time of westward expansion in the United States. Typically, simulations include directions or requirements for steps the students must take as they "act out" or simulate an event. This helps to ensure that student attention is focused on important understandings and skills, while still leaving room for student contribution and creativity.

Skills—Skills are the actions students should be able to perform or demonstrate as the result of a lesson, a series of lessons, or a unit of study. There are many categories of skills important to student learning. Some of those categories (with examples of skills in each) are *basic skills* (reading, writing, computing); *thinking skills* (synthesizing, summarizing; creating, defending a point of view, examining evidence); *production skills* (planning, setting goals, evaluating progress, asking important questions); *skills of a discipline* (map reading in geography, recognizing tones in music, interpreting metaphorical language in language arts); and *social skills* (listening, empathizing, considering multiple perspectives on an issue, taking turns). When identifying the skills students should master in any unit, lesson, or lessons, teachers should be aware of both the categories of skills and the specific skills. Teaching those skills explicitly is at least as important as teaching information explicitly.

Thinking maps—These are visual representations of ideas that allow a student to "unpack" their thinking and organize ideas in a visual format rather than solely in sentences or paragraphs. Thinking maps can be used with the whole class or small groups to construct meaning, or by individuals to plan writing, projects, or other tasks. Thinking maps can also be helpful as an assessment tool for teachers as they examine how students are thinking about particular topics or ideas.

Think–Pair–Share (T–P–S)—This instructional strategy, developed by Frank Lyman (1992), is used to engage all learners in thinking and talking about a question or issue important to a current area of study. Typically, the teacher begins a T–P–S by posing an important thought question. Students are asked to write their ideas or think about the question, working silently until the teacher calls time (usually two to three minutes). This is the thinking phase of the process. In the second phase, pairing, students turn to a peer and exchange their thoughts about the question. In the final phase, sharing, the teacher restates the question for the class as a whole and leads the class in a discussion of the question. The Think–Pair–Share strategy increases the likelihood that all students will engage with the question, will have something to contribute to the final discussion, and will be more invested in the outcome of the discussion than they would have been if the question had simply been posed once to the entire class and answered by the first student to raise a hand.

Tiering—Tiering is a process of adjusting the degree of difficulty of a question, task, or product to match a student's current readiness level. To tier an assignment, a teacher 1) determines what students should know, understand, and be able to do as a result of the task; 2) considers the readiness range of students relative to these goals; 3) develops or selects an activity that is interesting, requires high-level thought, and causes students to work with the specified knowledge, understanding, and skill; 4) determines the complexity level of that starting-point task compared with the range of student readiness; 5) develops multiple versions of the task at different levels of difficulty, ensuring that all versions focus on the essential knowledge, understanding, and skill; and 6) assigns students to the various versions of the task at levels likely to provide attainable challenge. To guide development of multiple versions of the task, a teacher may use the continua of the Equalizer (*see* **Equalizer**), use supporting materials that range from basic to advanced, provide forms of expression that range from very familiar to very unfamiliar, or relate the task to experiences that range from very familiar to very unfamiliar.

Resources on Differentiation and Related Topics

Armstrong, T. (1994). *Multiple intelligences in the class-room*. Alexandria, VA: Association for Supervision and Curriculum Development.

Aronson, E., Blaney, N., Stephin, C., Sikes, J., & Snapp, M. (1978). *The jigsaw classroom*. Beverly Hills, CA: Sage Publications.

Black, H., & Black, S. (1990). *Organizing thinking: Book one*. Pacific Grove, CA: Critical Thinking Press & Software.

Campbell, L., Campbell, C., & Dickinson, D. (1996). *Teaching and learning through multiple intelligences*. Needham Heights, MA: Allyn & Bacon.

Cohen, E. (1994). *Designing groupwork: Strategies for the heterogeneous classroom* (2nd ed.). New York: Teachers College Press.

Cohen, E., & Benton, J. (1988). Making groupwork work. *American Educator, 12*(3), 10–17, 45–46.

Cole, R. (Ed.). (2001). *More strategies for educating everybody's children*. Alexandria, VA: Association for Supervision and Curriculum Development.

Daniels, H. (1994). *Literature circles: Voice and choice in the student-centered classroom*. York, ME: Stenhouse Publishers.

Day, J., Spiegel, D., McLellan, J., & Brown, V. (2002). *Moving forward with literature circles: How to plan, manage, and evaluate literature circles that deepen understanding and foster a love of reading*. Jefferson City, MO: Scholastic, Inc.

Erickson, H. (2002). *Concept-based curriculum and instruction: Teaching beyond the facts* (2nd ed.). Thousand Oaks, CA: Corwin Press.

Gardner, H. (1993). *Multiple intelligences: The theory in practice*. New York: Basic Books.

Gardner, H. (1997). Reflections on multiple intelligences: The theory in practice. *Phi Delta Kappan, 78*(5), 200–207.

Gartin, B., Murdick, N., Imbeau, M., & Perner, D. (2003). *Differentiating instruction for students with developmental disabilities in inclusive classrooms*. Arlington, VA: Council for Exceptional Children.

Heacox, D. (2002). *Differentiating instruction in the regular classroom: How to reach and teach all learners, grades 3–12*. Minneapolis, MN: Free Spirit Publishing, Inc.

Hoffman, B., & Thomas, K. (1999). *Multiple intelligences: Teaching kids the way they learn, grade 3*. Torrance, CA: Frank Schaffer Publications, Inc.

Hyerle, D. (2000). *A field guide to using visual tools*. Alexandria, VA: Association for Supervision and Curriculum Development.

Kiernan, L. J. (Producer/Writer). (1997). *Differentiating instruction* [Video staff development series]. Alexandria, VA: Association for Supervision and Curriculum Development.

Kiernan, L. J. (Producer/Writer). (2000). *Differentiated instruction* [Web-based professional development course]. Alexandria, VA: Association for Supervision and Curriculum Development. Available at http://www.ascd.org/framepdonline.html.

Kiernan, L. J. (Producer/Writer). (2001). *At work in the differentiated classroom* [Video staff development series]. Alexandria, VA: Association for Supervision and Curriculum Development.

Kiernan, L. J. (Producer/Writer). (2001). *A visit to a differentiated classroom* [Video staff development series]. Alexandria, VA: Association for Supervision and Curriculum Development.

Kiernan, L. J. (Producer/Writer). (2003). *Instructional Strategies for the Differentiated Classroom* [Video staff development series]. Alexandria, VA: Association for Supervision and Curriculum Development.

Lyman, F. (1992). Think–Pair–Share, Thinktrix, Thinklinks, and Weird Facts: An interactive system for cooperative thinking. In N. Davidson & T. Worsham (Eds.), *Enhancing thinking through cooperative learning* (pp. 169–181). New York: Teachers College Press.

Nottage, C., & Morse, V. (2000). *Independent investigation method: A 7-step method of student success in the research process.* Kingston, NH: Active Learning Systems.

Parks, S., & Black, H. (1992). *Organizing thinking: Book two.* Pacific Grove, CA: Critical Thinking Press & Software.

Sharan, S. (Ed.). (1999). *Handbook of cooperative learning methods* (2nd ed.). Westport, CT: Greenwood Press.

Silver, H., Strong, R., & Perini, M. (2000). *So each may learn: Integrating learning styles and multiple intelligences.* Alexandria, VA: Association for Supervision and Curriculum Development.

Sternberg, R. (1988). *The triarchic mind: A new theory of human intelligence.* New York: Viking Press.

Sternberg, R. (1997, March). What does it mean to be smart? *Educational Leadership, 54*(6), 20–24.

Strachota, B. (1996). *On their side: Helping children take charge of their learning.* Greenfield, MA: Northeast Society for Children.

Taba, H. (1971). *A teacher's handbook to elementary social studies; an inductive approach* (2nd ed.). Reading, MA: Addison Wesley.

Tomlinson, C. (1995, Spring). Deciding to differentiate instruction in middle school: One school's journey. *Gifted Child Quarterly, 39*(2), 77–87.

Tomlinson, C. (1996). *Differentiating instruction for mixed-ability classrooms: An ASCD professional inquiry kit.* Alexandria, VA: Association for Supervision and Curriculum Development.

Tomlinson, C. (1998, November). For integration and differentiation choose concepts over topics. *Middle School Journal, 30*(2), 3–8.

Tomlinson, C. (1999a). *The differentiated classroom: Responding to the needs of all learners.* Alexandria, VA: Association for Supervision and Curriculum Development.

Tomlinson, C. (1999b). Leadership for differentiated classrooms. *The School Administrator, 56*(9), 6–11.

Tomlinson, C. (1999, September). Mapping a route toward differentiated instruction. *Educational Leadership, 57*(1), 12–16.

Tomlinson, C. (2000, September). Reconcilable differences: Standards-based teaching and differentiation. *Educational Leadership, 58*(1), 6–11.

Tomlinson, C. (2001). *How to differentiate instruction in mixed-ability classrooms* (2nd ed.). Alexandria, VA: Association for Supervision and Curriculum Development.

Tomlinson, C., & Allan, S. (2000). *Leadership for differentiating schools and classrooms.* Alexandria, VA: Association for Supervision and Curriculum Development.

Tomlinson, C., & Eidson, C. (2003). *Differentiation in practice: A resource guide for differentiating curriculum, grades 5–9.* Alexandria, VA: Association for Supervision and Curriculum Development.

Tomlinson, C., & Kalbfleisch, L. (1998, November). Teach me, teach my brain: A call for differentiated classrooms. *Educational Leadership, 56*(3), 52–55.

Tomlinson, C., Kaplan, S., Renzulli, J., Purcell, J., Leppien, J., & Burns, D. (2001). *The parallel curriculum: A design to develop high potential and challenge high-ability learners.* Thousand Oaks, CA: Corwin Press.

Tompkins, G. (1998). *50 literacy strategies step by step.* Upper Saddle River, NJ: Prentice Hall.

Wiggins, G. (1993). *Assessing student performance: Exploring the purpose and limits of testing.* San Francisco: Jossey-Bass Publishers.

Wiggins, G., & McTighe, J. (1998). *Understanding by design.* Alexandria, VA: Association for Supervision and Curriculum Development.

Wilhelm, J. (2001). *Improving comprehension with think-aloud strategies.* Jefferson City, MO: Scholastic, Inc.

Winebrenner, S. (1992). *Teaching gifted kids in the regular classroom: Strategies and techniques every teacher can use to meet the academic needs of the gifted and talented.* Minneapolis, MN: Free Spirit Publications.

Winebrenner, S. (1996). *Teaching kids with learning difficulties in the regular classroom: Strategies and techniques every teacher can use to challenge and motivate struggling students.* Minneapolis, MN: Free Spirit Publications.

Also helpful:

Exemplars K–12 (http://www.exemplars.com) is a source for standards-based, tiered lessons with rubrics and student examples in mathematics, science, reading, writing, and research skills. Contact Exemplars, 271 Poker Hill Road, Underhill, VT, 05489.

HOTT LINX (http://hottlinx.org) is an online source for differentiated units, lessons, and instructional strategies, K–12.

Index

Note: References to figures are followed by the letter *f*. References to samples are followed by the letter *s*.

INDEX

195

Differentiating Instruction (video), ix
Differentiation in Practice: A Resource Guide for Differentiating Curriculum, Grades 5–9 (Tomlinson & Eidson), x
discovery learning, 147
discussions, one-on-one
    as preparation for whole-group discussion, 29
    during small-group activities, 50, 52, 138
discussions, small group
    as informal assessment, 24, 29, 35, 138, 176
    for lesson closure, 114
    mixed-ability, and reading groups, 12f
discussions, student-led, 165, 169, 170–172, 173–174, 176–180, 181s, 182s, 183s
discussions, whole-class
    applications and, 147
    differentiating questions during, 26, 50, 56
    eliciting evaluative thinking during, 83
    eliciting generalizations during, 25, 52, 74, 75, 76, 84, 137, 139, 142
    informal assessment during, 24, 29, 35, 138
    introducing unit objectives in, 29, 31, 50, 73–74, 146, 164
    for lesson closure, 106, 108, 109
    List–Group–Label format, 102–103
    peer learning during, 104, 148, 177
    pre-assessments and introductory material, 46–47
    promoting critical thinking through, 31
    read-alouds and, 78–79, 107, 110, 165, 172, 173
    as review, 31, 35, 50, 54, 78, 104, 142

elementary classrooms, student characteristics in, x
Equalizer, 184–185f
ESL (English as a second language) students
    and differentiated learning contracts, 72, 87s–92s
    benefited by routine lesson openings, 27
    pairing strategies, 46, 52, 81
    and advance lesson preparation, 169
    tiered writing prompts and, 52, 76
    visual cues for, 34
exit card, 112, 117, 185
flexible grouping, 7, 185–186

games
    in instruction, 136
    review, 112–113, 115
Gardner, Howard, 186
Gardner's multiple intelligences
    defined, 186
    self-selected assignments and, 47–48, 85, 116, 143–144
    self-selected products and, 81–82
gender-based differentiation, 186
generalizations
    defined, 186
    eliciting, during discussions, 25, 52, 74, 75, 76, 84, 137, 139, 142
    in homework, 137, 154s
    posting in the classroom, 136, 154s
graphic organizers, 50, 62s, 84, 93s
grouping, flexible. *See* flexible grouping

heterogeneous groupwork. *See* mixed-ability grouping
homework
    interest-based differentiation in, 142
    readiness- and interest-based differentiation in, 135
    readiness-based differentiation in, 137, 139, 141, 147, 154s
How to Differentiate Instruction in Mixed-Ability Classrooms (Tomlinson), ix

IEPs. *See* individualized education plans (IEPs)
Improving Comprehension with Think-Aloud Strategies (Wilhelm), 168, 173
individualized education plans (IEPs)
    and differentiated learning contracts, 72, 87s–92s
    readiness-differentiated assignments and, 139, 141, 151
Instructional Strategies for the Differentiated Classroom (video), ix–x
intelligence preference, 186. *See also* multiple intelligences; Sternberg's triarchic intelligences
interest-based differentiation
    about, 9–10
    and anchor activities, 45
    and assessment, 118–119, 124s
    cross-subject motivation, 12f
    defined, 186
    and differentiated products, 151
    and homework, 135, 142
    importance of considering, 151
    interest surveys, 95–96
    in journal writing, 167, 174, 178–179
    and learning contracts, 72–73, 87s–92s

interest-based differentiation (*continued*)
    and RAFT activities, 118, 123s
    and small-group projects, 13f, 51, 54, 175
interest centers, 186–187
interest self-inventory, 95–96
interpersonal/intrapersonal intelligence, 48, 144
I Spy (game), 104, 187

Jigsaw, 52, 145, 187
journal writing
    prompts, 107, 169
    student choice in, 167, 174, 178–179

kinesthetic learners/intelligence, 27, 83–84, 108–109, 116, 143
knowledge rating scales, 101–102, 120s

language fluency issues. *See* ESL (English as a second language) students
leadership, in small groups, 105
Leadership for Differentiating Schools and Classrooms (Tomlinson & Allan), ix
learning centers
    defined, 187
    interest centers, 186–187
    readiness-based differentiation in, 22, 23, 28, 38s
    record-keeping, 23
learning contracts, 72–73, 87s–92s, 187
learning goals, 7–8
learning modalities. *See* intelligence preference
learning profiles. *See also* intelligence preference
    about, 10
    and anchor activities, 45, 146, 155s
    and differentiated products, 55–56, 77–78, 81–82, 149, 151
    importance of considering, 151
    mixing, in pairs and small groups, 12f, 30–31, 32
    and RAFT activities, 85
    and reading buddies, 12f
    and self-selected assignments, 47–48, 85, 116
learning stations
    defined, 187
    mixed-ability groupings and, 49–50
    student "experts" and, 48
learning style
    defined, 187–188
    and self-selecting activities, 118, 123s
    surveys of individual, 96
List–Group–Label, 102–103, 188
literacy skills, 17
logical/mathematical intelligence, 48, 85, 116, 144

About the Authors

Carol Ann Tomlinson, Ed.D, is Professor of Educational Leadership, Foundations, and Policy at the University of Virginia and was a public school teacher for 21 years. In 1974, she was Virginia's Teacher of the Year. During Carol's time in public school, she taught in many differentiated classrooms and directed district-level programs for struggling and advanced learners. Today, as co-director of the University of Virginia Summer Institute on Academic Diversity, she works with an international community of educators committed to academically responsive classrooms.

Carol has authored several books for ASCD, including *How to Differentiate Instruction in Mixed-Ability Classrooms, The Differentiated Classroom,* and (with Caroline Cunningham Eidson) *Differentiation in Practice: A Resource Guide for Differentiating Curriculum, Grades 5–9.* She consulted on and authored facilitator's guides for ASCD video staff development sets and developed ASCD's Professional Inquiry Kit on Differentiated Instruction.

Carol can be reached at the Curry School of Education, The University of Virginia, P.O. Box 400277, Charlottesville, VA, 22904, or e-mail cat3y@ virginia.edu.

Caroline Cunningham Eidson, Ph.D, is Director of Curriculum and Instruction at Triangle Day School in Durham, North Carolina, and an educational consultant focusing on curriculum development, curriculum differentiation, and the needs of advanced learners.

Caroline has taught children in differentiated classrooms in grades K–8 in both public and private schools. She cofounded Peabody School, a school for intellectually advanced children in Charlottesville, Virginia, and served as both a lead teacher and an administrator. She has also taught in the University of Virginia's Northern Virginia Master's Program in Gifted Education, supervising degree candidates during their teaching internships.

Caroline has provided workshops and certification training at the local, state, and national levels regarding curriculum differentiation and the characteristics and needs of gifted learners. She has several publications in the field of gifted education to her credit and is the coauthor (with Carol Ann Tomlinson) of *Differentiation in Practice: A Resource Guide for Differentiating Curriculum, Grades 5–9.*

Caroline can be reached at 3511 Carpenter Pond Rd., Durham, NC, 27703, or e-mail ceidson@nc.rr.com.

Related ASCD Resources: Differentiated Instruction

Audiotapes

Building a Place to Learn: Classroom Environments and Differentiated Instruction by Carol Ann Tomlinson (#202132)

Help for Your Struggling Learners: Strategies and Materials that Support Differentiated Instruction by Char Forsten, Betty Hollas, and Jim Grant (#202214)

CD-ROM and Multimedia

ASCD Professional Inquiry Kit: *Differentiating Instruction for Mixed-Ability Classrooms* by Carol Ann Tomlinson (#196213)

Networks

Visit the ASCD Web site (http://www.ascd.org) and search for "networks" for information about professional educators who have formed groups around topics like "Differentiated Instruction" and "Multiple Intelligences." Look in the "Network Directory" for current facilitators' addresses and phone numbers.

Online Professional Development

Available on the ASCD Web site:
   Online Tutorial: *Differentiating Instruction* (http://www.ascd.org/frametutorials.html)
   PD Online Course: *Differentiating Instruction* (http://www.ascd.org/framepdonline.html)

Print Products

ASCD Topic Pack: *Differentiating Instruction* (#101032) (also available online from the ASCD Web site: http://www.ascd.org)

The Differentiated Classroom: Responding to the Needs of All Learners by Carol Ann Tomlinson (#199040)

Differentiation in Practice: A Resource Guide for Differentiating Curriculum, Grades 5–9 by Carol Ann Tomlinson and Caroline Cunningham Eidson (#102293)

How to Differentiate Instruction in Mixed-Ability Classrooms (2nd ed.) by Carol Ann Tomlinson (#101043)

Leadership for Differentiating Schools and Classrooms by Carol Ann Tomlinson and Susan Demirsky Allan (#100216)

Videotapes

At Work in the Differentiated Classroom (3-tape series, plus Facilitator's Guide) (#401071)

Differentiating Instruction (2-tape series, plus Facilitator's Guide) (#497023)

Instructional Strategies for the Differentiated Classroom (4-tape series, plus Facilitator's Guide) (#403330)

A Visit to a Differentiated Classroom (videotape, plus Online Viewer's Guide) (#401309)

For additional information, visit us on the World Wide Web (http://www.ascd.org), send an e-mail message to member@ascd.org, call the ASCD Service Center (1-800-933-ASCD or 703-578-9600, then press 2), send a fax to 703-575-5400, or write to Information Services, ASCD, 1703 N. Beauregard St., Alexandria, VA 22311-1714 USA.